*The Emotionally Intelligent Pastor* is a timely and crucial book. We all know that the emotional and relational challenges of ministry can significantly contribute to ministry stress and pastoral burnout. Jeannie Clarkson has given pastors and other Christian leaders a superb guide to increasing emotional intelligence to avoid ministry stress and thrive in ministry.

—Russ Gunsalus, executive director of Education and Clergy Development, The Wesleyan Church

What an entertaining and enormously practical book! It begins with an engaging narrative of three pastors approaching their own emotional intelligence development challenges from different perspectives. The last half of the book turns to four components of EI and sixteen specific but simple habits a pastor can work on to become more self-aware, self-controlled, insightful to others, and a master interpersonal communicator. I can't say enough about the potential impact of this book. It is realistic, offering pathways to improvement we can work on for a lifetime. It will serve as a hedge against burnout and a catalyst for emotional and spiritual renewal. I will not only read it again for my own growth but will keep a copy handy to pass on to colleagues.

—Robert A. Moore Jr., DSL, international director, Freedom Outreach Ministry to the Military

*The Emotionally Intelligent Pastor* should become a standard text for all pastors, as well as anyone in ministry. For the future of Christ's church, may these skills become as essential to our call as learning sound biblical preaching!

—Julie Parsell, pastor of Christ Lutheran Church (OH)

Jeannie addresses this vitally important topic of emotional intelligence in a clear, understandable, and transparent way that challenges me to take a closer look at myself and my relationships. We are called to be "human beings" before we are "human doings," with fruitful partnerships flowing out of fulfilling fellowship with God and people. We have drifted from the Lord's original intent for leadership to be rooted in a loving heart being transformed by the Holy Spirit but I am thankful for Jeannie and others that he is raising up to remind us that eternal results come from healthy, Christ-like leaders and communities!

—Allan Pole, DMin, pastor of New Beginnings Church (Calgary)

This is an informative and enjoyable book to read and will be of value to pastors, church leaders, and anyone who wants to be more effective in leadership and in life. Not only will you gain a clear understanding of EI, you'll also gain practical insights and skills to help you apply it in real-life situations. Jeannie understands ministry, leadership, and emotional intelligence, and combines her formal training and extensive experience in ways that will help you apply EI in your personal and professional lives. This is one of those books that you'll be referencing time and time again.

—Gary J. Oliver, PhD, is the executive director of The Center for Healthy Relationships and professor of psychology and practical theology at John Brown University (AR)

Based on groundbreaking research, *The Emotionally Intelligent Pastor* provides valuable insights to help clergy navigate the stressful dynamics and complexities of ministry. Readers who embrace and practice the truths presented in this book will gain a much deeper understanding of themselves and the people they serve.

—Mark O. Wilson, author, pastor, and professor at Southern Wesleyan University (SC)

# The Emotionally

# Intelligent

# Pastor

## A GUIDE FOR CLERGY
## AND OTHER CHURCH LEADERS

...............................

Jeannie Clarkson, PhD

Copyright © 2019 by Jeannie Clarkson
Published by Education and Clergy Development of The Wesleyan Church,
Thriving Clergy, and Wesleyan Publishing House
Indianapolis, Indiana 46250
Printed in the United States of America
ISBN: 978-1-63257-338-4
ISBN (e-book): 978-1-63257-339-1

Library of Congress Control Number: 2019947025

Disclaimer: This book is not intended to offer professional or medical advice, and is not a substitute for professional or medical care. Some names and identifying details have been changed to protect the privacy of individuals.

Scriptures, unless otherwise indicated, are from the Holy Bible, New International Version. NIV. Copyright 1973, 1978, 1984, 2011 by Biblica, Inc. Used by permission of Zondervan. All rights reserved worldwide. www.zondervan.com

Scripture quotations marked (KJV) are taken from the Holy Bible, King James Version.

Scripture quotations marked (MSG) are taken from *The Message*. Copyright © 1993, 1994, 1995, 1996, 2000, 2001, 2002. Used by permission of NavPress Publishing Group.

Scripture quotations marked (NASB) are taken from the *New American Standard Bible*®, Copyright © 1960, 1962, 1963, 1968, 1971, 1972, 1973, 1975, 1977, 1995 by The Lockman Foundation. Used by permission.

Scripture quotations marked (NLT) are taken from the Holy Bible, New Living Translation, copyright © 1996, 2004, 2007, 2013 by Tyndale House Foundation. Used by permission of Tyndale House Publishers, Inc., Carol Stream, Illinois 60188. All rights reserved.

# Contents

# Introduction

In 1989, I was a licensed minister and pastor's spouse—and I was stressed to the breaking point.

Our congregation was worshiping in an unconventional building that had residential tenants living on the upper floor. Odd perhaps, if we were working in the United States (US), but not so strange in our overseas assignment ministering to US military personnel and their families off-post. Our tiny "parsonage" connected to a worship center our church shared with another flock.

Unfortunately, one upstairs tenant didn't appreciate the loud, pounding worship music that routinely emanated from the other congregation's services. Consequently, during the entire worship service, this renter would purposely (and angrily!) bang on the pipes above our apartment. Specifically, he banged on the pipes directly over the only chair available to me during the other congregation's weekly service!

This passive-aggressive behavior happened regularly. The situation escalated and became increasingly nerve-wracking. Externally, I developed a stress-induced rash. Internally, I wrestled with the question, Is this what the ministry is supposed to be like?

Your story is likely different from mine. You might not have to listen to clanging pipes early in the morning or all hours of the night. However, it might be that you would *gladly* swap whatever you're facing—continual criticism, resistance to change, unrealistic expectations, or the tense conflicts that are all too common in "church world"—for one simple noisy neighbor!

Let me ask: What's your ministry version of an angry, pipe-banging tenant? What's the problem you face that keeps getting louder and more exasperating? Do you find yourself asking questions like: Is this what ministry is supposed to be about? How did I get here? How long can I keep doing this?

Here's what we know is true: some pastors are thriving. They're not only making a difference for the kingdom of God, but they're finding their efforts rewarding and satisfying. They're loving life!

Meanwhile, another group of pastors is having a radically different experience. They're finding the ministry so unrewarding and unsatisfying, they're leaving in droves each year. The numbers are shocking. The stories are heartbreaking. Each situation is unique, but two common themes are *stress* and *burnout.*

I wrote this book for every pastor—young and old, inexperienced and seasoned, those who are prospering and simply want to sharpen their leadership skills and those who are discouraged and on the verge of quitting, and everyone in between.

My goal is to show you some startling research and help you understand a few, very powerful leadership skills. These practices—if cultivated and employed proactively—can help you avoid some ministry frustrations altogether. Used in response to existing problems, these skills are remarkable correctives. I have seen them make happy leaders even healthier and more effective! I've also seen them help weary leaders recover a sense of balance and joy. Almost like a vaccine, these practices have been shown to protect pastors against burnout and pave the way to transformational leadership.

Even if you are a pastor who is doing pretty well right now, my desire is to help you sharpen your self-awareness, people skills, and relational abilities. I want to help you leverage the good things that are happening right now in your ministry for even greater things.

But first, a disclaimer: If you are looking for a book of flashy quick fixes or foolproof ministry hacks, this is not that book.

I'm reminded of John Wooden, legendary UCLA basketball coach in the 1960s and '70s. Wooden led the Bruins to seven straight national championships (and ten in twelve seasons). No other team or coach has come close to equaling these records.

Former players still talk with amusement about how Coach Wooden would use a portion of the team's first practice each season to show his players the proper way to put on their socks and lace up their sneakers! Why? Because he knew that one bad blister could sideline a player for days. So, before teaching tricky zone defenses or practicing fancy passes, he ensured that his team had mastered this vital but often overlooked skill.

In some ways, the contents of this book—developing emotional intelligence—probably seems obvious, elementary, and even old-fashioned. So be it. Because here's what is true: only by learning such rudimentary concepts and skills—what makes you tick (and what ticks you off), self-mastery, and how to read people and situations—can you become effective in ministering to others. Like right-fitting basketball socks and shoes, emotional intelligence can keep you in the game—and off the ministry sidelines.

Because of my dual experience in pastoral ministry and in counseling hundreds of people, including clergy, I'm now convinced that successful, satisfying ministry rests on two fundamentals. The first is connecting with God and following his call. The second is connecting with people—understanding *yourself* so that you are able to relate wisely with others and influence them for eternity. This book is all about that second fundamental.

Hear me again: This book is not a challenge to imitate the ministry program of some other church or pastor. This is a roll-up-your-sleeves look at what it means to be emotionally intelligent.

It's a timely topic. The church, particularly the Western church, finds itself at a challenging moment in history. We stand at a crossroads between the familiar, traditional church that has flourished for most of the last fifty years, and the unknown form of church God is taking us toward as we seek to minister to a rapidly morphing culture. Like never before, we need healthy, self-aware leaders who have heard from God and who are equipped to come alongside people, love them well, and take them to new and better places.

I commend you for your desire to develop the critical set of emotional and relational skills known as *emotional intelligence*.

Shall we get started?

## PART 1

# The Pain and Problems of Pastors!

# Meet Susan, Bill, and Jim

Susan, Bill, and Jim glanced absent-mindedly at their menus and made small talk—sharing travel anecdotes, making comments about the swanky host hotel, and speculating about Clayton's whereabouts.

Soon after a young, impeccably dressed waiter brought their drinks, Jim's phone dinged. He checked it, frowned, and stared blankly at his companions. "Looks like Clayton won't be joining us after all."

"For dinner?" Susan asked.

Jim shook his head. "For the whole conference. In his words—and I quote: 'Sudden church emergency.'"

Bill groaned loudly. "Isn't that just like the ministry? You look forward to a getaway for *months*. Then at the last possible second, something—or someone—torpedoes your plans. Brutal."

The others nodded knowingly. Susan abruptly raised her glass of water, "To Clayton. God bless him!"

"Here, here . . . to poor Clayton!" the other men said, grabbing their drinks to join the impromptu tribute. After a few seconds, Susan leaned forward and lowered her voice, "I know this is Chicago, not Vegas, but am I correct in assuming that we're operating by the old 'whatever is said here, stays here' rule?"

"Absolutely," Jim replied. "We pastors need settings like this, if for no other reason than to have a place to let down our hair." Then rubbing his mostly bald head, "Not that I have that much left to let down . . . hair, I mean."

Susan smiled broadly. "I knew I liked you guys right from the start! Okay then, true confession: I actually turned off my phone at 5 p.m. yesterday for that very reason. I didn't want to risk getting one of those calls. I needed to get out of Dodge or else . . . , if you know what I mean—and I think you do."

Jim and Bill laughed heartily.

Then Jim, in keeping with his type A, take-charge personality, called the waiter over to take their orders. Afterward he said, "Okay, how about this, while we wait on our fifteen-dollar gourmet hamburgers. The conference organizers put us in these groups and asked us to meet before tomorrow's opening session to get acquainted. How about it? Susan, tell us about yourself. You mentioned getting out of Dodge. Does that mean you're from Kansas?"

Susan laughed. "Funny, I *do* live in Kansas. But not Dodge City. I'm a new pastor at an older church in rural Claymore, Kansas. Little town of 2,700 people. I actually grew up here in Illinois. I'm married to an overworked, underpaid high school basketball coach. We do not have children . . . not yet, anyway. Mark keeps saying, 'Babe, I've already got fifteen boys I can't keep up with!'

"As far as hobbies, hmmm, I like to bike. And I've been doing some family genealogy lately. Don't tell anyone, but I think I might actually be a distant cousin of Benedict Arnold."

The men laughed. Jim asked, "New pastor, huh? So what's that like?"

Bill interrupted, "No, no, Jim! Remember the ground rules? No shoptalk tonight. Our assignment was just to get to know each other. We're supposed to save all our bellyaching for tomorrow."

Jim smiled. 'You're right. You're absolutely right! See there, I can go from zero to sixty *broken rules* in less than 4.3 seconds! You guys better watch me like a hawk. Okay, what about you, Bill? Give us a quick bio. You got any traitors in *your* family tree?"

Bill shook his head, while swallowing a sip of tea. "No traitors that I know of. Matter of fact, I grew up in a very patriotic military family. So

I've lived all over. But Nashville is home now—coming up on thirteen years. Longest I've ever lived in one place."

"Nashville? Really?" Susan sounded wistful, almost envious. "Wow. Music City . . . I bet you have some killer worship at your church."

Bill smiled. "I can confirm that there is no shortage of talented musicians within a ten-mile radius of our church." He paused, and continued, "I have also learned that talent and flakiness seem to be directly proportional."

Susan and Jim laughed. Then Susan whispered loudly, "Still, I would *gladly* trade you three un-flaky church members for one talented singer. Whaddya say?"

"That's very tempting. Let me mull that over. Now, where was I?"

"Nashville," Jim said.

"Of course, Nashville. Thirteen years. Before that, I was an associate pastor for about a decade in North Carolina. I am married to Celeste, my high school sweetheart. She has a very successful cupcake business." Bill patted his gut and added, "Can you tell?

"She and I are empty nesters. Twin sons—one is newly married and the other has zero desire to settle down. So, no grandkids yet."

"What do you do for fun?" Susan asked.

"Fun?" Bill responded in mock ignorance. "I know I've heard that word before. Remind me what it means? No, seriously, I don't know. I play golf. Badly. At least once a year. I actually used to fish and read a lot. Lately I don't have the energy for either. Celeste accuses me of having a mistress named Netflix. But that's enough about me. What about you, Jim?"

"My turn already? Okay, let's see. Back in the nineties I had a growing software company, but I kept feeling a pull toward vocational ministry. So I finally sold the company and went to seminary. Took a church in Dallas. We were there for nine years. Good years. *Great* folks! Saw tremendous growth. Then we got the call to go to Denver."

Jim paused, took a drink, and cleared his throat. "Been there now for a year. *Big* suburban church . . . ." He paused and pursed his lips. Susan and Bill could almost see the wheels turning in his head. He wanted to say more, and he finally did.

"A *big* church with *big* problems that I *really* wish someone had told me about eighteen months ago—but, I know, I know. We're not supposed to get into all that 'professional stuff' tonight, so let me get back to the personal." He took a sip, swallowed, and continued.

"I'm a couple months away from hitting the big 5-0. Not so sure how I feel about that. My wife, Rebecca, and I just celebrated our twenty-fifth anniversary. We have a son who's a freshman at UT. We have a daughter in tenth grade.

"Like you, Susan, I enjoy cycling. Genealogy, not so much. Probably because I'm too afraid of what I might dig up! But I do like to get on my bike. I actually did my first mini-triathlon a few weeks back. I'm thinking all that intense training is probably what's kept me sane the last couple months. I guess we can talk more about all that tomorrow."

The burgers arrived. The consensus was that, while they *weren't* worth fifteen dollars, they beat airport food hands down. The new friends laughed and shared more about their childhoods and families. About 7:45, they settled up with the waiter, and Jim said, "I need to answer some e-mail. But, hey, this has been fun. I'm glad they put us in a group together. l look forward to talking about our ministries tomorrow. Maybe the two of you can help me figure out what to do with a certain—ah, never mind. Tomorrow, right?"

Laughing, they got in one of the downtown hotel's ornate elevators together. One by one they exited.

Back in Room 418, an exhausted Bill talked briefly to his wife, Celeste. Afterward, he flipped on the TV. By 8:15, he was snoring, remote control still in his hand.

In Room 603, Susan worked up the courage to check her messages and voicemails. No crises! She breathed a sigh of relief and opened her fancy conference workbook. She read with interest the updated list of breakout seminars being offered the next two days—especially one entitled "Leadership Challenges for Women in Ministry."

In Room 1226, Jim unpacked, did his customary forty-nine push-ups (one for every year of his life). After a shower, he opened his laptop and answered thirty-six emails. At 10:47, he set his alarm for 4:45 a.m.—so he could get in an early morning run—and turned out his light.

The next morning—following a plenary session that featured uplifting music and an inspiring message on emotional intelligence for pastors, Susan, Bill, and Jim met up, grabbed some coffee, and plopped down in three comfy chairs in a far nook of the massive hotel's lobby.

After sharing some thoughts on the morning gathering, Jim suddenly grinned broadly. He rubbed his hands together and announced, "At last. Finally! Now we get to talk about the juicy stuff." He glanced at the instruction sheet they'd been given and read aloud: "'Have each group member briefly share: (a) his/her reason for attending the conference, (b) one pressing ministry frustration, and (c) one known area of needed personal/spiritual growth.'

"Not that I'm eager to talk about 'ministry frustrations,'" Jim said, making air quotes while he winked at his new friends, "but do you two mind if I go first?"

"The floor is all yours," Susan replied with a smile.

"Okay, I uprooted my family and moved to Denver—because the board at my new church told me they wanted *change*. They looked at my resume, history in business, and track record at my previous church and saw that I'm a high-energy leader. I like to get things done. 'You're exactly what we need,' they said. 'You're just the leader to get us unstuck and moving in a good direction.' So it seemed a perfect fit."

A cloud came over Jim's face. "One year in, and we haven't done diddly-squat. I'm banging my head against the wall—or maybe I should say, against *Greg*." Jim's voice was starting to rise slightly.

Susan's eyes widened. "Who's Greg?"

"A very influential board member . . . and a big donor."

"So what's Greg doing—or not doing—to frustrate you?"

Jim explained, "Let me back up and say that most of the board—and our key ministry leaders—are fully on board with my vision. Or it seemed like they were. But right when we got consensus on a plan and started the ball rolling, Greg balked. In our meeting two nights ago, he did a total about-face: 'I'm not so sure. I feel like we're moving too fast. I've talked to a number of other members who have reservations.'"

Susan and Bill noticed Jim's voice was controlled but his jaw was tight. His face was starting to flush.

Bill chimed in, "So, how'd you respond?"

Jim's expression changed. He looked glumly down at the floor and kicked at the marble floor with his boot. "Not great. I could have—should have handled that situation a lot better. All this took place right at the end of the meeting. Greg started in, and what can I say? I sort of went off on him. Then I told the board, 'Looks like you have a decision to make' and walked out the room."

Susan's mouth fell open at the same time that Bill's eyebrows rose. Jim noted their expressions and said, "Exactly. Not my best moment. I've had a few phone conversations since. Swapped some texts and emails. But obviously, I've got work to do when I get home from this conference. Meanwhile, I need to learn how to deal more effectively with people who don't want to change and who frustrate the heck out of me. A little 'emotional intelligence' maybe for the pastor who sometimes acts like an emotional idiot?"

Susan and Bill asked a few questions, and the more things Jim got off his chest, the calmer he got.

Finally Bill nodded empathetically. "Jim, for what it's worth, if I had a dollar for every time I've overreacted in board meetings and put my big foot in my even bigger mouth, I'd be on the *Forbes* list. Let me jump in here, take the spotlight off you, and say a little about my situation.

"Like I said last night, I have been at my Nashville church for almost thirteen years now. We've done okay—most folks would say pretty well.

Our membership was about 325 when I arrived. It's about 400 now. Got a small but good staff. Faithful volunteers. Thankfully, a supportive board. No financial issues to speak of. But personally? Y'all, I don't know how else to say it. I am *out of gas*. It's all I can do most weeks to pull a Sunday sermon together, and lately I've even been getting comments about my preaching. Thank God for an associate pastor who is well-liked and great at pastoral care!"

Bill sighed and continued. "Celeste—my wife—is really worried about me. She's actually the one who heard about this conference and insisted I come. Especially when she saw the emphasis on pastors who are dealing with stress and burnout.

"So there you have it. The ugly truth is I'm fifty-five and I dread going into the office most days. Honestly, I'm wondering how much longer I can hang in there. That's why I'm here."

Jim and Susan fell silent as they looked at their colleague who was clearly weary.

Finally, Jim asked softly, "So, is this all a recent thing? Or have you been dealing with this for a while?"

Bill took off his glasses and cleaned them with his napkin. "It's probably been a long time coming. A combination of things. I'm a workaholic, always wanting to fix or save everybody. Ha, I'm on the job sixty-plus hours a week trying to keep everybody happy—and they're still not happy!"

Susan whistled softly. "Whoa. I've only been at this ministry stuff for a few months, but even *I* know that's a bad combination."

"Tell me about it," Bill nodded. "Celeste would say I'm a people pleaser. And she's right. I can't tell people 'no.' So I have few healthy boundaries. And I avoid conflict like the proverbial plague.

"Case in point. Celeste has been on me about not spending enough time with her. So, just the other week I said, 'Let's go out for a nice dinner.' So she gets excited and makes dinner reservations for a Thursday night.

"Well, wouldn't you know it? The Tuesday before our fancy date, one of my council members informs me that the Boys & Girls Club that our church sponsors is having their awards ceremony on Thursday night. I tell him, 'I'm sorry; I have plans.' He says, 'Bill, this has been on the church calendar for months.' I say, 'I never saw it.' He says, 'Look, this is a *big* deal. You need to be there to recognize some community members who are big donors.' So, I cave.

"Then I spend the next twenty-four hours fretting about how I'm going to tell Celeste. She's been looking forward to this date for a solid week. She keeps mentioning it. So when I finally break the news to her on Wednesday night, she bursts into tears. Story of my life. Saying yes to everybody but my family.

"And that's not the end of it! Get this. After the ceremony, I get home and that same council member has the nerve to call me and chew me out for forgetting to mention the club's newest board member! How am I supposed to know they have a new member? Apparently I can't read minds very well!"

Bill sighed heavily. "Whatever. I have tried so hard to please these people! I can't win for losing. And I'm to the point now where, honestly, I hardly care anymore."

Susan asked quietly, "Bill, have you ever had a sabbatical?"

He looked incredulous at her. "You're joking, right? I've never even had a two-week vacation where I really got to completely unplug. I get to the beach, and I'm staring at the gulf with a cell phone glued to my ear, counseling somebody back home!"

There was a long silence. Lots of nodding and pursed lips. "Well," Jim suggested hopefully, "maybe this conference will give you—give us all—some good, practical help over these next couple days."

"I sure hope so," Bill said wistfully. "That would be a much-needed blessing. OK, enough of my sob story. What about you, Susan?" He glanced at his sheet, "Why'd you come? What's frustrating you? What are you hoping to get out of this conference?"

"Wow, I hardly know what to say. You guys shared a lot. This is good. For perspective, you know? Maybe I shouldn't feel so badly about my little church in Kansas? I was thinking I was the only one struggling . . . but then I hear your stories. Guys, you have my word. I will keep you both in my prayers.

"This is my first church, first ministry assignment. My undergraduate degree was in English. I taught for a couple years, but then I felt called to ministry, so I went back to divinity school.

"I just love to see people using their spiritual gifts. I love to help believers grow in the faith and steadily become disciples and leaders. I believe that's the way the church grows.

"Some of my denominational friends warned me that this church might be difficult. I just kept seeing all this potential. It's a small rural church with a lot of family generations. A few younger couples from nearby communities have started attending recently."

Susan paused and sighed heavily. "But I'm confused. I'm six months in—and definitely in over my head. People are nice enough, but they don't seem to understand my approach. They're standoffish. I feel like they view me with suspicion and mistrust. A couple of the older members have even made comments about 'remembering when *men* were the ones leading God's church.'

"I came this week because I want to grow in my leadership. I am a continual learner. I need help figuring out how to work with these people, how to gain their trust."

Jim scratched his head. "So it sounds like they view you as an outsider who wants to change 'the way we've always done things around here.'"

Bill nodded. "And if they're traditional—it might take them a while to get used to the fact that you're a woman. But they'll warm up. You've got a pastor's heart—that's obvious. They'll eventually see that."

"Any ideas for how I can speed up that process?"

"Probably by doing exactly what you did last night with us. Spend time with them. Listen to their stories. Tell them your story. Laugh and cry with them. Let them see you're human. I would guess a lot of those folks are not nearly as educated as you. They might feel intimidated."

The trio continued talking, asking questions of one another, sharing frustrations, and offering encouragement. Finally it was time for the pre-lunch breakout sessions.

As they stood up to go, Bill asked, "We've got a full day in front of us. Y'all want to get together in the morning here at the hotel restaurant for an early breakfast and debrief session?"

Jim smiled, "I was planning to do my morning run, but honestly, I think visiting with you two would be the healthier choice. I'm in."

"Sounds good," Susan said.

# Why Are So Many Pastors Struggling?

Recently while in a meeting with a group of pastors, I asked the question, "What is your number one problem in pastoral ministry?" One wise guy in the audience blurted out, "People!" Instantly the room filled with laughter and nodding heads.

This pastor simply expressed what every minister feels at times. It's not that we don't like people. In truth, people are the reason we went into ministry in the first place! However, we know all too well that people go off the rails and create drama. That's true of some people all the time and all people some of the time. When they do, they leave plenty of dysfunction, tension, and mess in their wake. Often, we are the ones asked to step in and help restore order and sanity.

With his jokey quip, my clergy friend was simply referring to the challenge of working with people. And it *is* a constant challenge.

## My Journey with Emotional Intelligence

Here's my own clergy story in brief. See if you can relate.

I was young when I first got the chance to preach to some small gatherings of military families—and even to some US soldiers in a German prison. During these experiences I felt God's hand upon me, and I began to sense a call into ministry.

In response to these stirrings I began extension studies toward a degree in Bible and also completed a ministerial internship. Before long I was not only a pastor's wife, I was also a licensed minister! My one desire was to please God and if that meant making sacrifices, so be it.

My husband and I lived in a German community, ministering primarily to American military personnel. It was rewarding, though the hardships of living in a different culture definitely wore on me. I felt isolated. I didn't really fit in with the locals, and sometimes I wasn't so sure I fit in with the military lifestyle either.

There were other pressures and stressors. As I mentioned in the introduction, financial strains prompted us to sublease the worship center to another church. This arrangement definitely helped with the bills—it did *not* help my mental health! We were sharing our kitchen and restrooms with an entire church—and the members didn't exactly grasp the concept of boundaries. Complicating matters was the fact that military congregations are always in flux, with soldiers getting reassigned on a regular basis. This constant turnover made us feel like every day was Groundhog Day—like we were starting over repeatedly!

When our upstairs tenant began his passive-aggressive pipe banging, I thought, *Is this what ministry is supposed to be like?* As I listened I imagined, *This must be what water drip torture is like.*

In truth, those clanging pipes overhead were a blessing in disguise. They functioned as a wake-up call. They were the impetus for my asking big questions about big issues. Even when we returned to the United States—and the outward clanging stopped, one question did not: Is that how the ministry is supposed to be?

I continued my biblical studies, continued observing churches and pastors. Though I saw many good things—changed lives, spiritual growth—I also observed other realities that concerned me at a deep level: countless pastors dealing with their own versions, large and small, of clanging pipes, and an alarming number of clergy burning out and walking away from vocational ministry.

It was oddly comforting to know that I wasn't alone in my "ministry struggles." At the same time, it was disturbing to see so many good-hearted ministry leaders trying to continue on fumes. Other questions bubbled up in my heart: Were the fulfilled pastors I knew less susceptible to discouragement because they were doing (or not doing) certain things? Is ministry burnout inevitable? Can it be avoided? These questions nagged at me, but I was still too busy to address them.

It was after completing my bachelor of biblical studies' degree that I felt a new call, one I never saw coming: counseling! It didn't take long to realize it was in my sweet spot. I completed a master's degree and started a Christian counseling center, which I still operate to this day.

As I continued to engage with other pastors and hear their unique clanging-pipe stories, the more I found myself wanting to help them. The old questions that had taken a back seat for a few years were still within me, but in a new form: What if we could help leaders develop the habits they need to be healthy and effective and stem the tide of clergy burnout? And, what if we could gain the skills needed to be more relevant to our church members and culture? More effective and influential in relating to others?

By this time I was in pursuit of my PhD in counseling psychology. As I pondered possible dissertation topics, someone suggested the idea of *emotional intelligence* (or EI). If you've read leadership books and articles, no doubt you've encountered this term or one of its many synonyms: cognitive empathy, emotional quotient (or EQ), emotional awareness, or emotional management. In simplest terms (a longer description follows in the next chapter), EI is the ability to understand the feelings and reactions of both yourself and others, and then to use this insight to skillfully avoid or solve relational problems.

I was intrigued. I read everything I could find on the subject and began wondering: Is this it? Do pastors who are emotionally intelligent actually experience greater success in managing the expectations of others and leading them toward an agreed-upon vision? And if so, might those EI-savvy pastors experience less frustration and a greater sense of accomplishment in ministry as a result? And wouldn't it follow that a greater sense of satisfaction and accomplishment serves to inoculate leaders from burnout or at least reduce the chances of it happening? It seemed to me that increased influence just might lead to decreased burnout. I knew I had to find out.

I thought about *role conflict* (often cited as a leading factor in clergy burnout). Role conflict refers to the stress or anxiety one experiences while attempting to juggle conflicting roles or competing expectations. Could it be that pastors with higher EI are able to manage role conflict more easily and therefore be less susceptible to burnout?

I kept talking with and listening to pastors. Some admitted deep struggles with insecurity and identity, confessing a continual, almost obsessive need to prove themselves and to avoid failure at all costs. I discovered this performance-based success orientation is common among high-achieving individuals—and among victims of burnout.

Of course, I didn't only want to help pastors who were struggling. Proactively I also wanted to give up-and-coming leaders the tools they need to thrive in ministry and to avoid altogether the pitfalls of burnout. And I wanted to come alongside effective leaders, to help them—in the words of the apostle Paul—"excel still more" (1 Thess. 4:1 NASB) by sharpening their relational skills.

My research was uncovering the truth that business leaders with higher EI enjoy greater influence and an increased ability to spearhead change and transform their organizations. When I found a couple of studies demonstrating the effect of higher EI on pastors, I concluded that perhaps I was on to something that would make a difference.

## *My Research Results*

My dissertation topic approved, I went to work. In the spring of 2013, I surveyed more than 250 pastors (263 to be exact) in the midwestern United States.

My research yielded three major findings: [1]

1. Pastors with higher EI scores reported less role conflict and less angst from trying to juggle the contradictory expectations of others—or contradictions between others' expectations and one's own values. The correlation was small, yet significant.
2. Pastors with higher EI scores experienced a greater sense of personal accomplishment. I found a large degree of correlation between EI and feelings of personal satisfaction. The data seemed to support my theory that a greater sense of accomplishment means less burnout.
3. Those pastors who tended to base their identity and worth on perceptions of success or failure in ministry reported higher rates of emotional exhaustion. I found a moderate degree of correlation between performance-based self-esteem and exhaustion. In other words, the more a pastor tends to base his or her worth on ministry performance, the more likely that pastor is to struggle with burnout.

What does this all mean? It means that a high degree of emotional intelligence helps leaders experience less frustration and more satisfaction and success—significantly reducing the chances of burnout.

That data convinced me that EI is key for becoming a transformational spiritual leader and—as a by-product—avoiding burnout.

Let me issue a disclaimer: I don't wish here to give the impression that pastoral leadership is harder than other kinds of leadership. Pastors surely aren't the only ones charged with setting direction, providing inspiration, and trying to keep everyone and everything moving toward a goal. I recognize that leadership of any organization is tough.

But as the great spiritual leader Moses could attest (remember his forty-year career of shepherding God's people from Egypt to the Promised Land in Exodus 12 to Deuteronomy 34?), pastoral leadership presents a unique set of challenges.

For one thing, how does one accurately measure soul growth? The success metrics for a church are very different from a business that simply looks at the financial bottom line.

For another thing, church is a voluntary association. The only ones getting a paycheck are the clergy and staff, meaning that pastors do not have the option of firing trouble-making parishioners. And the pastor's pay, for the record, isn't always great—though the hours are always long. The point? Though running a business and shepherding a congregation are both challenging, ministry leadership uniquely tests the resourcefulness, character, and relational acumen of a leader.

## *Five Common Leadership Challenges*

Since completing my PhD, I've continued my reading, research, and interaction with pastors. In fact, I have identified five common leadership challenges. Leaders who learn to navigate these wisely—EI-savvy leaders—are able to grow their influence. Those who do not gain EI often succumb to burnout because of these issues. Grim, but true.

So what are the most common challenges that pastors must learn to navigate?

### Criticism

To be sure, every leader experiences criticism. That comes with the territory. And here we're not referring to constructive criticism, which actually is a great gift (see Ps. 141:5). We're talking about a steady stream of hateful, hurtful comments. This kind of unrelenting verbal attack and mean-spirited criticism, all too common in some churches, can zap a pastor's energy and wound him or her to the core. Learning to handle criticism is crucial.

### Conflict

The research shows that conflict is one of the main reasons pastors leave ministry.[2] Many pastors get sick and tired—literally—of the constant fighting between individual church members, factions within the church, and pastors and board members. Conflict resolution skills are a must.

### Unrealistic and Conflicting Expectations

Unrealistic and conflicting expectations may take out more pastors than anything else. Consider what people want from their pastors: The older generation wants hospital visits on a regular basis. The younger folks want more activities that appeal to them and their children. Another group believes the pastor should be a more efficient administrator. Some want a contemporary service, while others want traditional worship. Oh, yes, don't forget the expectation that the pastor be a powerful preacher like John Piper, John MacArthur, or better yet, the apostle John. How about a charismatic personality? And did we mention the various programs that the denominational leadership wants implemented?

One pastor asked his board to make a list of all the things they each felt he should be doing. He gathered the lists, compiled them, and then reported back: fulfilling everyone's expectations would only take him 114 hours a week![3]

Trying to meet everyone's typically unrealistic and conflicting expectations is deadly. Learning to manage expectations is imperative.

### Resistance to Change

How many leaders have you known who were passionate about their vision for a congregation and excited about the direction God was calling them? How many times have you seen those same pastors a year or so later, deflated and discouraged because even the slightest hint of change resulted in a tidal wave of protest? Again, as the biblical experience of Moses demonstrates, people are resistant to change—even good and needed change. It is upsetting for most people. This dynamic wipes out a lot of pastors. It is difficult to be tenderhearted and thick-skinned at the same time, but healthy and effective clergy must learn to lead through change.

### Stress

There is the constant strain of being on call 24/7. Then there's the pressure of knowing that people can reach you around the clock and around the calendar. Add **ST**rain to p**RESS**ure and you get **STRESS**!

Many pastors wear multiple hats and juggle a variety of responsibilities. Many are bivocational. This kind of overwork ruins a lot of good-hearted clergy. Some might say, "Aw, what did you expect? Of course the ministry is stressful! Eternal matters are at stake! Suck it up and do what Paul said: 'Endure suffering . . . as a good soldier of Christ Jesus' (2 Tim. 2:3 NLT)." To that I say that the high rate of pastors who are suffering from a kind of spiritual PTSD (post-traumatic stress disorder) is unacceptable! Pastors need help learning how to deal more effectively with stress and all the other common clergy killers.

## *Losing PEP*

What happens when a pastor does not learn how to face these challenges in healthy ways? The pastor is likely to lose his/her

- **P**hysical health
- **E**motional energy
- **P**astoral effectiveness

Maybe you have felt such things? Perhaps you can relate to what Abraham Lincoln expressed in the midst of the Civil War when he allegedly sighed, "Sometimes I think I am the tiredest man on earth."

Losing your PEP can mean being physically weary, spiritually depleted, mentally exhausted, emotionally drained, relationally spent, or some combination of all of these.

### Physical Health

A 2010 study of 1,726 United Methodist clergy showed that they had higher rates of diabetes, arthritis, high blood pressure, angina, asthma, and obesity than their North Carolina peers.[4] Other studies have linked excessive stress to an increased risk of cardiovascular disease and diabetes. Add to this finding the fact that Christian ministers as a group are notorious for their poor eating and exercise habits. Bill, from our story in chapter 1, could benefit immensely from putting down the cupcakes and the remote and putting on his walking shoes.

If you find yourself battling chronic ailments, stress could be one of the causes!

## Emotional Energy

If there is one thing pastors need, it's energy—the more the better! Unfortunately, stress has been shown to reduce emotional—as well as mental and physical—energy. One larger survey showed that pastors also reported a loss of passion when they were facing excessive conflict, criticism, or resistance to change.

## Pastoral Effectiveness

In my own research, when I saw that only 2.5 percent of the more than 260 pastors I surveyed reported feeling "greatly satisfied in working with people,"[5] I felt deeply disturbed!

So what is the solution? How can we equip clergy to meet these challenges that cross cultural boundaries and denominational lines and that regularly destroy the PEP of good-hearted pastors worldwide?

The good news is that while we can't eliminate the obstacles, we can help leaders develop a set of skills that make them stronger and more resilient in the face of criticism, conflict, resistance to change, unhealthy expectations, and stress. And we can help them acquire habits that will lead to greater influence and life-transforming ministry.

The skills that I am speaking of have proven effective among secular business leaders and clergy alike. They are the skills or habits of emotional intelligence.

## PART 2

# The Promise and Power of Emotional Intelligence

# What Is
# Emotional Intelligence (EI)?

As planned, pastors Susan, Bill, and Jim met for breakfast in the hotel restaurant on the second morning of the Chicago pastors' conference.

"The chicken and waffles look pretty good," Bill muttered as he closed his menu. "But I should probably practice a little *dietary* intelligence to go with all the emotional intelligence we're learning."

"Yeah," Susan interrupted. "What do you old pros think about all this stuff? In my last year of divinity school, a professor suggested I read Goleman's book on emotional intelligence. I bought it, but never read it."

Bill laughed, "Wait a few years. Your stack of unread books will be like mine—about thirty feet high."

Jim nodded, "I bet at least three of my church members hand me a new book every month: 'Pastor, you've *got* to read this!'"

Susan persisted, "I wish three of my members would *speak* to me each month! But, really! There's something to this EI stuff, right?"

"I do think that," Jim agreed. "Now, anyway. I didn't for a long time. Back in my business days, people used to forward me articles about EQ or EI from *Forbes* and other magazines. At first I rolled my eyes and thought, *Yeah, that's what we need—to sit around the office and get in touch with our emotions and sing 'Kum Ba Yah.'*

"But then I realized, EI's not about being 'touchy-feely'. It's just about being self-aware and people smart. It's common sense, really. Yet it's very *uncommon*. God knows I've got plenty of work to do."

Bill and Susan nodded.

In simplest terms, emotional intelligence (EI) can be defined as the ability to (1) understand the ways people (including you) feel and react, and (2) use this knowledge to wisely avoid or smartly solve relational problems.

EI has been described in all sorts of ways:

- Rare self-knowledge combined with rare people skills
- A keen awareness of one's own inner state, a sensitivity to what others are feeling, and the ability to use all that insight to navigate relational challenges
- Being in tune with the moods of others or able to sense the vibe in a group
- Developing a kind of emotional X-ray/relational radar system that anticipates and addresses potential problems
- Intentionally and empathetically tuning in to others—their fears, frustrations, longings, or expectations
- The ability to size up people and figure out what makes them tick—not in order to take advantage of them but to better relate to them and serve them

What does emotional intelligence look like in everyday life? People with high EI do the following sorts of things:

- A college professor—following a class member's death—dispenses with her planned lecture and encourages students to share how the event has affected them.
- A dad notices that his nine-year-old son is unusually quiet and says, "Hey, you want to go up to the playground and shoot some baskets?"
- A sales manager senses obvious tension in the air during a weekly sales meeting and decides to "name the elephant in the room."

◉ A pastor gets a harshly critical, grossly unfair email from an influential church member, so he bangs out an angry response—then hits Delete instead of Send.

◉ Following a shake-up at a small software company, the new COO holds a series of brown-bag lunches with anxious employees to explain new procedures and protocols.

◉ A pastoral candidate candidly tells a church search committee, "I know many pastors' wives enjoy prominent, high-profile ministry roles. You need to know that's not my wife's personality, gifting, or desire."

## A Brief History of Emotional Intelligence (EI)

Probably everyone has heard the term IQ or *intelligence quotient*. It was coined by German psychologist William Stern in 1912. During the early part of the twentieth century, researchers developed IQ tests that measured such things as abstract and verbal reasoning ability, spatial reasoning, and memory skills. A person's IQ is a score derived from their results on such a standard intelligence test.[1]

But there have always been those who have maintained that IQ isn't the only game in town and have insisted that there are ways to be smart other than simply "book smart." In 1920, it was Edward Thorndike, an American psychologist, who introduced the idea of *social intelligence*. He described this as the capacity to nimbly navigate social relationships. In other words, he was saying, some are "people smart."[2]

In 1983, Howard Gardner, a Harvard professor and psychologist, proposed the idea of *multiple intelligences*—specifically, he identified seven distinct ways people are smart:[3]

1. Visual-spatial intelligence—having artistic or architectural acumen; being "picture smart"

2. Bodily-kinesthetic intelligence—understanding movement and physical activity; being "body smart"
3. Musical intelligence—aptitude for music; being "music smart"
4. Interpersonal intelligence—skill in interacting with others; being "people smart"
5. Intrapersonal intelligence—understanding oneself; being "self-smart"
6. Linguistic intelligence—using language effectively; being "word smart"
7. Logical-mathematical intelligence—reasoning and calculating ability; being "number smart"

Around the same time in 1983, Robert Sternberg was advocating his *triarchic theory* of intelligence, which focused on analytical, creative, and practical intelligence. Within his category of practical intelligence, Sternberg included both intrapersonal and interpersonal aspects of intelligence.[4]

What we're calling *emotional intelligence* sprang from all these early conceptualizations of intelligence that involved social intelligence and intrapersonal and interpersonal aspects of intelligence.

In 1990, Peter Salovey and John D. Mayer defined *emotional intelligence* as "the ability to monitor one's own and others' feelings and emotions, to discriminate among them and to use this information to guide one's thinking and actions."[5] Thus they combined both cognitive and emotive aspects of intelligence in their theory.

Daniel Goleman (the author mentioned above by Pastor Susan) explored this idea of emotional intelligence with his bestselling 1995 book entitled *Emotional Intelligence: Why It Can Matter More Than IQ.* More than anyone else, he brought the concept of emotional intelligence out of the academic realm and into the common vernacular.

Meanwhile, in the academic realm, fierce debate ensued about whether emotional intelligence should be considered a trait/ability or a skill. A trait or an ability is considered fixed or innate and somewhat determined. Considering EI a skill would suggest that it can be learned and developed. The Salovey/Mayer model was an ability model. Goleman's was deemed a skill model—in other words, EI is not an innate talent but a learned or developed capability. Others explained EI using aspects of each viewpoint and were termed *mixed* models.[6]

Emotional intelligence assessments were then developed according to these various models. Testing ensued to determine if it is possible to benefit from EI training programs.

## A Model of Emotional Intelligence for Pastors

I developed my model based on Goleman's four basic domains of emotional intelligence: self-awareness, self-management, social awareness, and relationship management.[7] I have renamed these four basic domains as Personal Insight, Personal Mastery, Relational Insight, and Relational Mastery. Emotionally-intelligent ministry flows from who we are and reaches out to others.

I have included skills and habits for each of these main domains that are similar to Goleman's sub-components, yet I have adjusted these to make them more applicable to the work of congregational ministry and other organizations. I call them both skills and habits to convey the idea that they are first skills to acquire, then habits to maintain.

I do not consider this list of skills and habits exhaustive but simply basic working points for utilizing emotional intelligence core concepts in the work of congregational ministry.

### Sixteen Skills and Habits of Emotionally Intelligent Pastors

| Personal Insight | Personal Mastery | Relational Insight | Relational Mastery |
|---|---|---|---|
| • Monitoring your emotions | • Resetting your mind-set | • Listening attentively | • Building trust |
| • Tuning in to self-talk | • Managing emotional triggers | • Tuning in to others | • Managing expectations |
| • Identifying emotional triggers | • Communicating directly | • Knowing your team | • Empowering others |
| • Asking for feedback | • Maintaining your passion | • Learning the landscape | • Managing conflict |

## *Business Emphasis on EI*

As the field of business discovered EI, countless research studies ensued, producing mountains of data. The results showed that emotional intelligence does matter greatly in corporate leadership. It is now universally accepted that executives and managers with higher emotional intelligence are better at cultivating productive relationships with their direct reports and more effective at creating and fostering teamwork, leading change, maintaining morale, and empowering followers toward innovation. In short, companies that employed leaders with higher emotional intelligence were more financially profitable.[8, 9]

EI is especially relevant today since most entities and organizations are moving away from the hierarchical leadership structures of the past to more team-based, democratic management styles. Relational acumen has never been more crucial. Simply telling people what to do no longer works, and business recognizes this fact.

For this reason, top corporations spend a great deal of money annually training their top leaders in emotional intelligence. They see this proactive investment as essential to a healthier bottom line. And sometimes the training is reactive—helping less effective leaders sharpen poor people skills.

## Neurobiology

What does science say? Is emotional intelligence a fixed ability that only a fortunate few are born with? Or is it a skill that can be learned and enhanced throughout life? In other words, does attending training programs increase emotional intelligence, or is it a waste of time and money?

Neuroscience is shedding light on these questions. Studies show that even in infancy, we begin demonstrating various levels of EI. Early childhood experiences—in particular, one's connection to one's parents—have been shown to make a big difference.[10] As is often the case, science suggests EI is less an either/or question (such as, nature vs. nurture) and more a both/and reality.[11, 12, 13] In other words, everyone has some level of emotional intelligence, but not everyone has the same amount or capacity, and emotional intelligence can be developed.

## EI and Church World

Emotional intelligence is not, as some allege, a bunch of psychological mumbo jumbo. And it's more than going in for counseling and getting all touchy-feely. EI is self-knowledge coupled with interpersonal skills. Despite the concerns of some, the field of emotional intelligence is in no way foreign to Scripture or antithetical to the Christian faith.

The Bible champions the idea of self-awareness, which is central to emotional intelligence. In Psalm 4:4 we read, "Tremble and do not sin; when you are on your beds, *search your hearts* and be silent" (emphasis added). In another place, the psalmist requests God's help in figuring out the motives behind his actions (see Ps.139:23). The Old Testament book of Proverbs says famously, "Above all else, *guard your heart*, for everything you do flows from it" (4:23, emphasis added). This ancient collection of wisdom goes on to commend the person who can insightfully read others, saying, "The purposes of a person's heart are deep waters, but one who has insight draws them out" (20:5).

The New Testament gospels depict Jesus as being tuned in to others. Multiple times he is said to be keenly aware of others—their thoughts, feelings, and barely perceptible actions (see Matt. 12:15; 16:8; 26:10; Mark 5:30; 8:17; John 6:61). He was an expert on the human heart and he came, the Bible tells us, to help the poor (see Luke 4:18).

One cannot read the Bible without coming to this conclusion: God desires for his people to be emotionally healthy and whole and to enjoy great relationships with one another.

I am convinced that it's time for spiritual leaders to heed the teaching of Scripture, to utilize the latest scientific and psychological research, and to pursue greater emotional health and strength for themselves and their people.

The good news is that if you are a leader, especially a spiritual leader, emotional intelligence can help you influence people for the gospel, which in the end is the only thing that matters.

## The Elements of Emotional Intelligence

The skill sets encompassed by the term *emotional intelligence* may be organized for purposes of analysis and discussion in several different ways. Many agree, however, that there are four components of emotional intelligence. These are the four ways in which highly emotionally intelligent people—in this case, pastors—excel:

1. **Personal Insight:** Highly emotionally intelligent pastors possess a better understanding of their own emotions than do others.
2. **Personal Mastery:** High EI pastors control and regulate their own emotions and reactions better than others.

3. **Relational Insight:** EI-savvy pastors read, understand, and empathize with the emotions and reactions of other people better than most.

4. **Relational Mastery:** Pastors with high emotional intelligence are better at emotional reasoning and more skilled at effective, persuasive communication than others.

All of us possess varying abilities and capacities in these four areas. We all have some degree of insight, self-control, and communication skill. However, people with high EI have honed these skills to a much higher level of competency.

It is true that some enjoyed the advantage of better nurturing in their youth to get a head start. However, that's not the most important factor. What matters most is that all these skills can be learned, and we can practice them until they become habits. You and I can improve in each of these four areas. By doing so, we increase our effectiveness at building strong relationships and influencing others.

How well you develop the skills of emotional intelligence and how habitually you employ them will determine your level of emotional intelligence and how effective you will be in leading and influencing others.

## *Toward Greater Emotional Intelligence*

Let's sum up what we've seen so far:

◉ Clergy and other leaders face five common problems—criticism, conflict, unrealistic expectations, resistance to change, and stress. Any of these (or all of them collectively) can kill a leader's health and enthusiasm. These realities are commonly cited as primary causes of pastoral burnout.

43

- ◉ The best strategy for negating the debilitating effects of these leadership challenges is to develop one's emotional intelligence to the highest degree possible.
- ◉ Emotional intelligence is a great asset in dealing with the pressures and pitfalls of ministry. Used proactively, it boosts one's ability to engage, inspire, and transform others!

What now? How do you—how does any leader of any entity—begin the process of developing greater emotional intelligence?

The biggest step of any journey is actually the step just before the first step: making the decision to go on the journey in the first place! For many, this can be scary. It means leaving all that is familiar. It means being stretched and forced to learn new things. It means venturing into the unknown. Journeys take time. They always have a cost.

On the other hand, if you seldom launch out, you routinely miss out. You miss the adventure of seeing and experiencing new things, seeing all the beautiful realities just over the horizon.

I hope you will decide to make this trip—all the way to the end. I hope you'll be willing to look into your own heart and ask yourself some potentially unsettling questions:

- ◉ Could I benefit from more insight into what makes me tick?
- ◉ Could I use more skill in interacting with others?
- ◉ If I don't change anything about my leadership style and relational habits, what are the chances I will find ministry fulfilling in five years? What are the chances I might end up a burnout statistic?
- ◉ Am I okay with being a so-so leader, or do I want to max out my leadership potential—becoming one who powerfully and positively engages, inspires, and helps shape those with whom I interact?
- ◉ Would I like to be healthier emotionally?

◉ Am I willing to wrestle with hard questions and do recommended exercises that lead to greater personal insight and relational effectiveness?

◉ Am I willing to seek and listen to feedback from others?

◉ Am I willing to allow the Holy Spirit to show me the truth about my heart and interpersonal skills?

◉ Am I willing to embrace the pain that accompanies all authentic spiritual and personal growth?

If you answered these questions honestly, my guess is you find within yourself the desire to begin the journey of transformational leadership. If so, get ready to see amazing things!

# What Difference Does Emotional Intelligence Make?

Susan, Jim, and Bill decided to sit together for the closing plenary session of the pastors' conference.

It was a panel discussion about the benefits of emotional intelligence and the risks of—I guess we could call it—*emotional illiteracy*. The panel consisted of a CEO of a Fortune 500 company, who was also a devout Christian; a former megachurch pastor who'd been through a spectacular scandal about four years previously; and an elder statesman/pastor who recently authored a bestselling book titled *Soft-Hearted & Thick-Skinned*.

The stories and anecdotes they told were sad and funny, wise and practical. The session had it all. It was a cautionary tale and an inspiration and a celebration of God's grace, all at once.

Susan scribbled furiously. Jim and Bill kept giving each other knowing looks and shaking their heads at how familiar it all sounded.

## Lack of Pastoral Job Satisfaction

As mentioned previously, in 2013, as part of my PhD work, I surveyed 263 pastors of various denominations on the topic of clergy burnout. During that process, I learned a great deal about both the pain and the passion of modern pastors.

Some of the findings were—and still are—alarming. Large numbers of clergy are stressed out, worn out, and dropping out. One ex-pastor, a victim of serious burnout, admitted feeling ill-prepared for the unique challenges of ministry:

My seminary experience was that I mostly learned information for the head, not wisdom for the heart. I learned how to exegete biblical texts but no one taught me to read human souls. I never had a single class in listening—which is one of the most important skills a pastor could ever develop. I never had lectures, much less whole courses, in "taking the temperature of a group," "watching over one's heart" (Prov. 4:23), or leading through change. My seminary graduated a lot of students who were Bible brilliant (and we knew it!), but how many of us were people smart? Some were socially awkward. Others were spiritually prideful— the church version of a genius physician with absolutely no bedside manner. Where was the intensive psychological work-up that showed a future pastor's strengths/ weaknesses, potential problem areas, etc.? Where were the workshops on dealing with angry people, depressed people, grieving people, controlling people? Where was the seminar on "expectations in church world"? Maybe seminaries do these kinds of things now, but mine surely didn't in the mid 1980s.

Many seminaries in recent years have corrected some of these shortcomings. Nevertheless, clergy continue to tell me that they felt inadequately prepared for the people challenges they experienced when they left seminary and entered congregational ministry.

Even among the clergy who are not on the verge of burnout, there is a lot of frustration and dissatisfaction associated with pastoral ministry. Many ministers, despite their fervent praying and faithful efforts, feel like they are just not making a difference—or at least not the difference they hoped they might make. They are stuck and they don't see a way to get unstuck and change the status quo.

This was one of the really eye-opening results of my own study. Less than 3 percent of the pastors I surveyed reported being highly satisfied in working with people and their ability to influence people. This prompts me to pause and ask, which group are you in—the tiny minority that is highly satisfied or the ministerial majority who are stuck, struggling, or worse?

To be fair, not all the research is discouraging. The pastors I surveyed are committed to Christ and his church. They want to be effective leaders. They are eager to grow in skill. A study by the Barna Group found that clergy as a whole are voracious readers who purchase, on average, three and half books per month![1] It's not clear if they're reading all those books, but they're buying them! Barna also discovered that of books purchased by pastors, one of the three main topics of interest is leadership.

While the bad news may be that you didn't learn emotional intelligence in seminary, the good news is that you can cultivate it now. And you must, because the evidence demonstrates that emotionally intelligent pastors are more effective—and consequently, more satisfied in ministry. They are also less likely candidates for pastoral burnout.

## Why Emotional Intelligence Matters

Think about the world we live in—the world to which we are called to minister. It is filled with people who are fallen and hurting. Sin—both the wrong we do and the wrong done to us—leaves us broken. This is why so many cry out to God and perhaps visit our churches.

But that's only one truth. Here's a second: hurt people hurt people. Broken people break other things. They not only create problems for themselves, they also wreak havoc in all their relationships. They even drag their baggage into church and create more drama!

There it only gets more complicated, because pastors—those who love God and people, who desire to see people reconciled to God, and who have been called by God to be ministers of reconciliation—are people too. Pastors are flawed and imperfect, just like everyone else. We are all works in progress.

So put all that together, and what do you get? Wounded people—prone to forget that pastors have their own struggles—forming congregations that harbor all sorts of unrealistic expectations and put inordinate demands on their leaders. And clergy who oftentimes, despite the best of intentions, forget and then crash into their own limitations. The result is often a perfect storm of legitimate needs, conflicting wills, and unholy desires—in short, relational chaos.

Do you see? Navigating the complexities of congregational life and pastoral leadership will take all of the wisdom and relational skill you can possibly acquire. By developing and sharpening your emotional intelligence you can avoid many of the common pitfalls of ministry. Poorly managed stress and congregational conflict have kept many good pastors from their best work—and even led to burnout. That doesn't have to be your story too.

Specifically, let me mention seven reasons EI matters—or you could say, seven ways I see emotional intelligence making an enormous difference in your life and work as a pastor:

## EI Can Be a Force of Transformation

Historians tell us that the famed nineteenth-century English preacher Charles Haddon Spurgeon battled serious depression. He would preach glorious sermons, then—stricken by dark moods—fall into bed for days at a time. Over time, however, Spurgeon came to see that his deep depression actually equipped him to minister more effectively. He concluded, "I would go into the deeps a hundred times to cheer a downcast spirit. It is good for me to have been afflicted, that I might know how to speak a word in season to one that is weary."[2]

Spurgeon's example reminds us of an important spiritual reality: God created us as emotional beings, and when we embrace—rather than deny—that truth, our emotions can become a force for our own transformation as well as a tool to help others.

At different points in our lives, we all struggle with powerful emotions: anger, anxiety, fear, or depression. Like a Category 5 hurricane, such strong feelings can be destructive. Unchecked, they can even ruin us. Or, we can become adept at realizing what's stirring in our hearts, give those emotions to God, and then ask him to use them to make us the people and servants he created us to be. In the thick of ministry, when we become aware of pride, insecurity, or envy, we can use those emotions to motivate us to repent more fully and trust God more deeply. We are then able to harness our emotions and leverage them for his kingdom.

And let's face it. We need some strong emotions, harnessed and channeled in good ways! After all, how much longer would the slave trade have lasted without the righteous anger of the abolitionists?

## EI Paves the Way for Greater Influence

Imagine having a supervisor (for example, a denominational leader or board chairman) who is moody and unpredictable. One week he or she is friendly; the next, because of some unforeseen circumstance, he or she is sullen and aloof. Imagine this unpredictable authority figure is also hypersensitive, defensive, volatile. and prone to go off on people—sometimes even on you! Or suppose this person is not a good communicator. You rarely know what he or she is thinking. You usually only find out about changes in plans long after the fact, and even then, only through the infamous grapevine.

Would you trust such a person? Would you see them as *for* you? Would you be inclined to enthusiastically follow their leadership?

We know the answers to these questions. Such a leader would *not* have your confidence—much less any kind of significant influence in your life. You would be guarded around such a leader. You may become anxious and ineffective in your job. You probably wouldn't take any type of initiative because you'd be forever fearful of setting him or her off!

This is a major reason emotional intelligence is so critical. It paves the way for us to enjoy greater influence with people. When we are stable, sensitive, and self-aware, others are drawn to us. We've said that hurt people have a tendency to hurt people. The flipside of that is that secure people—leaders who are secure in their identity—create secure environments. When a pastor is truly secure in the love of Christ, he or she presides over a staff, board, or church culture in which everyone feels safe, instead of living in fear and walking on eggshells.

### EI Can Reduce or Even Prevent Stress and Burnout

We've touched on this already, but emotional intelligence gives pastors the tools they need to address all the most stressful ministry problems they face: criticism, conflict, wrong expectations, and resistance to change.

Without the healthy insight and people skills that come from EI, ministers are like soldiers going out to battle with no protective gear or ammunition! Minor criticism can cause mortal wounds. Small conflicts can turn into fierce firefights. The thought of leading change can be enough to make wounded and weary pastors go AWOL!

### EI Offers Practical Help for Conflict Management

Contrary to the old saying, death and taxes are not the only certainties in life. We can add conflict to that short list. Unfortunately, conflict pervades church life.

I'll go ahead and let you in on a secret: I hate conflict. In fact, I spent a good portion of my life trying to avoid it.

The problem with avoiding conflict, however, is that it doesn't go away. It simply goes underground—only to resurface later, usually at the worst possible time and place.

Through the years I have gotten better at managing conflict—probably because I've had so many opportunities to practice! The happy result? When I've managed conflict well, rather than avoiding it, it has greatly reduced my stress levels!

Conflict can be managed, leveraged for growth, and sometimes prevented. Emotionally intelligent pastors who learn to manage conflict will reduce their overall stress, enjoy their ministry more, and develop more overall effectiveness and influence.

## EI Can Spare Us the Miseries of Unrealistic Expectations

Only four months into their marriage, Pastor Susan and Mark were still like honeymooners. They'd hardly had a disagreement. Then they entered their first holiday season.

Susan was filled with nostalgic anticipation. She couldn't wait to open presents on Christmas morning at her parents' home with her new husband, then eat her family's big annual feast. Meanwhile, clueless, good-hearted Mark was filled with similar excitement—preparing his big Christmas surprise for Susan—flying to snowy Colorado on Christmas Eve for a romantic holiday ski trip! You can guess the outcome!

Both Susan and Mark had clear expectations of how they would do Christmas. They learned the hard way about the importance of not just having expectations, but stating, discussing, and clarifying them ahead of time.

In the ministry, this same *expectations dynamic* is always at work with pastors and congregations. Consciously or not, both parties bring expectations, verbalized or not, into the relationship. Leadership gurus refer to these expectations as "the psychological contract." By this they mean an implied agreement between two interdependent parties, either individuals or groups, in a working relationship. Even when a written agreement or contract or job description seeks to spell out these specifics, people often interpret these contracts differently.

Where do such expectations, whether of pastors or parishioners, come from? They are the result of stated agreements, passing conversations, and prior experiences, as well as personal assumptions, values, and beliefs. EI-savvy leaders learn to identify and monitor these ever-present realities.

## EI Enables a Pastor to More Effectively Lead Change

On a trip to Florida to visit children and grandchildren, I left my phone in a public place. By the time I realized my mistake and returned—just minutes later—the phone was gone.

I transferred my cell service to a nicer replacement phone. Still, I felt vaguely distressed. This reaction surprised me until I realized what was going on—I wanted my old phone back! I missed its sparkly silver case and the way it felt in my hand. It was almost as if I was leaving a part of myself behind. I was more attached to my phone than I knew!

This experience reminded me that all change—even minor, positive change—is unsettling. Change often brings with it a sense of loss. For many it raises potentially scary questions about an unknown future.

No wonder some people resist change so fiercely—we don't like surprises. Most of us prefer predictability, certainty, and routine. These constants help us feel like we have some measure of control.

Guess what? All these realities hold true in church world too. People cling tightly to their religious traditions, even if those practices are only cultural preferences and not biblical commands. Every new pastor has probably heard congregants refer to "the way we do things around here."

All of this explains why spiritual leaders must understand the psychological dynamics—the emotions of change. This insight is indispensable in creating buy-in. For even when people perceive a change as for the better, they often still feel anxious about it! As James Emery White has written, "People will not even consider change unless they are impacted on an emotional level."[3] It's no wonder that in one study, successful turn-around pastors scored higher in emotional intelligence.[4]

EI leaders understand these realities and learn to adjust to them.

## EI Contributes to Greater Health

Many pastors I talk with report feeling lonely. Although they are constantly ministering *to* people and surrounded *by* people, pastors—especially solo pastors of smaller congregations—fill a solitary role that tends to set them apart. Parishioners misunderstand men and women "of the cloth," and view them as different from regular people. Many wrongly perceive pastors as not needing anyone.

This situation is exacerbated by the numbers of pastors who not only experience limited connection inside the church but also struggle to find time and energy to forge friendships outside the church. All this leads to a sense of isolation in ministry. H. B. London, head of pastoral ministries for Focus on the Family, says that 70 percent of pastors report that they have no friends.[5]

This is problematic because recent studies show that loneliness reduces our immune system response.[6] In other words, being healthily connected with others not only supports emotional and spiritual well-being, but physical health as well. Imagine that. Deep connection with others can reduce the occurrence of the common cold! (Of course, hand sanitizer doesn't hurt either.)

Pastors with higher EI understand the danger of isolation and the wisdom of being in community. They make self-care a high priority—engaging in important spiritual disciplines like solitude and Sabbath.

They find hobbies that replenish them. They set healthy boundaries in relationships and with regard to work. They work at resolving conflict in healthy and biblical ways. All of these things together contribute to their emotional—and yes, their physical—well-being.

## The Big Promise of Emotional Intelligence?

Put all those realities together and here is what the research—and experience—demonstrates conclusively:

*Greater emotional intelligence leads to reduced stress and increased influence.*

Given this promise, it would seem that emotional intelligence would be prized by leaders in the church even more than leaders in business. But the truth is that church world lags behind in the development of emotional intelligence. This needs to change.

Leading an all-volunteer organization toward a collaborative goal requires more relational finesse than leading any business. Business leaders can insist on compliance with the threat of a pink slip or the promise of a paycheck. Leaders in churches and other nonprofits have to rely on character and trust, relational capital, and a compelling vision.

Leading a congregation—in which some members have more longevity and greater influence than the pastor—is complicated and tricky. Think of it: assorted ages, varied backgrounds, diverse personalities and expectations—it is definitely more art than science. Effective leadership hinges much more on character and people skills than advanced degrees, cool org charts, or detailed job descriptions.

And given that many congregations hire the pastors they want to lead them, we have to ask: Who really is the leader? Is it the church that calls the pastor and has the authority to fire him or her? Or is it the pastor who leads the people? This odd arrangement, this ambiguous balance of power, the many unclear and often unstated expectations—can you see the immense need for emotional intelligence and relational expertise?

Again, the research bears out the importance of EI. The pastors who were best able to lead congregational growth as well as those who were better able help "turn around" declining churches had higher emotional intelligence scores.

## What It Takes to Cultivate Emotional Intelligence

Before we turn our attention to how to develop the four primary components of EI, let me mention three prerequisites to cultivating emotional intelligence.

### A Growth Mind-Set

A growth mind-set is the first prerequisite to change. What is a growth mind-set? It's being open to looking at yourself, your emotions, and your relationships in new ways. You have to be willing to face hard—and in some cases, unpleasant—truths about yourself. You have to be willing to challenge yourself to try new things and be open to new learning experiences. Only this kind of courageous openness and vulnerability will produce change.

Yet most of us don't like facing our flaws. We are reluctant to try new things. We avoid examining our feelings and thoughts. We want to play it safe and stay in our comfort zone.

All these things fly in the face of seeking to develop emotional intelligence. If you want to cultivate EI, you will have to be willing to experience the anxiety of change. All growth requires change, and all change is uncomfortable. Every achievement of your life to date required you to be open to new ideas and experiences. It also meant embracing the discomfort of change. Growing your emotional intelligence is no different.

## A Willingness to Take Action

As mentioned previously, you cannot simply read about emotional intelligence and expect to develop it. Learning the concepts and practical applications of emotional intelligence is foundational, yet insufficient.

You must commit to doing the exercises. Remember the old saying, "Neurons that fire together wire together?" It's true. Doing the exercises in the upcoming chapters will help you personalize the principles. It's the only way to turn mere intriguing ideas into transforming habits.

## An Unwavering Commitment

Only serious commitment enables us to apply wisdom to ourselves and to our relationships. Commitment means regular practice and application—for the long haul—even when we don't feel like it. It means following a plan that can slowly but surely turn into a lifestyle. It means sticking with a program long enough to turn conscious, clunky actions into unconscious, smooth habits.

**PART 3**

# Developing the Skills of Emotional Intelligence

# Gaining Personal Insight

We all have lightbulb or "Aha!" moments from time to time—sudden realizations where things that had previously been fuzzy or even invisible crystallize for us and come into focus.

Bill had one of those moments while packing his bags in his hotel room following the closing session of the conference. He did his customary double-check of the closet and the bathroom to make sure he didn't leave anything behind. Then, unconsciously, he began straightening the hotel room. He wiped off the bathroom counter and put his used towel, hand towel, and washcloth in a handy pile by the tub. He gathered up all his empty water bottles, food wrappers, and other trash—even picking up some chip crumbs off the carpet. He put the TV remote back in place and carefully restacked all the magazines on the coffee table by the sofa. Next, he moved the extra pillows on the floor back onto his unmade bed. It was then that he thought, *Wait, what am I doing? Why do I feel a compulsion to straighten my hotel room when a maid will be coming to clean it in a couple hours?*

His behavior bugged him all the way to the airport. He thought about comments his wife had made—especially when he'd recently canceled their dinner date. Slowly a realization began to settle over him—a painful, uncomfortable truth: *Much of what I do in life, I do because I'm a people pleaser, off the charts. I'm afraid of what others will think. I don't want anyone being unhappy with me—not even someone whom is paid to provide a service!*

It was an epiphany, for sure, and at first it made Bill feel disgusted with himself. But thanks to what he'd learned at the conference, he caught himself. He stopped flogging himself mentally. Slowly, a seed of resolve began to form: *I'm not ignoring this. I'm going to address this internal quirk of mine.*

### What Is Personal Insight?

Personal insight is self-knowledge. It conveys the idea of seeing into oneself. Often termed *self-awareness*, it means to grow in our awareness of our feelings, thoughts, motivations, and the impact our behavior has on others. Personal insight is grasping who we are, how we are wired, and what makes us tick. It's what we gain as we follow Socrates' ancient dictum to "know thyself." It is the ability to understand ourselves, as well as how others perceive us.

Are you an introvert or an extrovert? Do you gravitate toward people or tasks? Do you have a good sense of how your past has contributed to the person you are in the present? Do you know your quirks and foibles, your strengths and weaknesses, your passions and your pet peeves? Have you identified your deeply ingrained biases and personal preferences? Are you clear on how you come across to others in various settings and situations? All these questions fall under the purview of personal insight.

The fact is, we need personal insight because we have blind spots. We're *not* able to see ourselves from the vantage point of others. Who would know they had a piece of parsley stuck between their front teeth without a good mirror or a good friend? This blind-spot reality probably explains, for example, why we're taken aback whenever we hear ourselves on audio or see ourselves on video—"Do I *really* sound/look like that?"

The great news is that everyone can grow in personal insight! It just takes desire, effort, and courage. The research says this is time and energy well spent. Emotionally intelligent pastors are better than others at recognizing their own moods, emotional triggers, and self-talk. They are more aware of their own emotional reactions to others. This is huge because it enables them to avoid being sucked into a lot of unnecessary, soul-draining drama. As a result, EI-savvy pastors have more personal energy—and it shows in how they come across to others.

Rather than denying or suppressing feelings—or being hijacked by them—high EI pastors gain information from their feelings. They use their emotions as gauges. As a result, they are continually growing in personal insight—how their moods, words, and deeds impact others. They continually engage in prayerful introspection. They seek an honest view of themselves and an accurate assessment of their strengths and limitations. They are not afraid of feedback. They seek it out. In fact, they insist on it.

## Do You Really Know Yourself?

We all have an innate hunger for self-understanding. We want to know who we are, who our ancestors were, and what our purpose or God's plan for us is. We have a need to make sense of our experiences.

Perhaps the question I hear more than any other in my counseling office takes multiple forms: Why do I do the things I do? Why do I keep ending up in the same kinds of relationships? Why can't I change? How can I get unstuck? Why does history seem to repeat itself? Do I have a sign on my forehead?

When we understand our histories, temperaments, beliefs, strengths, and limitations, and when we grasp how all these factors have come together to shape who we are—then and only then can we make greater sense of our lives. Only then can we answer the question of why we act, react, and relate the way we do.

## The Formula for Gaining Personal Insight

Two key components are needed if we are to grow in personal insight: personal reflection and feedback from others. We might express this idea in a simple formula:

**Personal Reflection + Feedback from Others = Increased Personal Insight**

For example, Pastor Bill was engaging in a lot of personal reflection leading up to the pastors' conference. No big surprise there. It was because he was struggling mightily. He was experiencing the truth of the old C. S. Lewis observation about God whispering to us in our pleasures but shouting to us in our pain.

It's true isn't it? There's nothing like difficulty in life to get our attention, to cause us to slow down and become introspective. The hard times force us to look within—and look up. Bill's weariness and the timing of the conference meshed perfectly (how good of our sovereign God!), giving Bill a fresh opportunity for self-reflection. I would simply remind you here that you don't have to wait for a crisis to make self-reflection a habit.

Bill's insight was also increasing thanks to his wife's faithful yet painful feedback. Remember what he told his pastoral colleagues at dinner: "Celeste would say I'm a people pleaser."

## The Lost Art of Self-Reflection

Healthy introspection is a lost art in our culture. Mention the importance of being reflective, and you'll get blank stares or protests about how such a contemplative lifestyle is all but impossible. Granted, if we fill our calendars with activity, and if we stay plugged into media 24/7, there's precious little time left over for simply being, thinking, and reflecting. And pastors aren't immune. Even in church world, the pace of life can be breakneck, and the never-ending list of events and programs can become all-consuming. The biblical Mary was described as thoughtful and contemplative, prone to ponder deep things (see Luke 2:19). Modern-day Marys are rushed and distracted, pulled in a thousand directions, and prone to ponder, "How will I ever get it all done?"

Hard as it may be, we have to cultivate self-insight. Socrates was right, "The unexamined life is not worth living." And an unexamined life is certainly not worth inflicting on others! We need to recapture the lost art of self-reflection. By that, I don't mean some kind of self-absorbed, New Age navel-gazing. I mean prayerful, Spirit-aided analysis.

King David modeled this courageous, humble practice when he prayed, "Search me, God, and know my heart; test me and know my anxious thoughts. See if there is any offensive way in me, and lead me in the way everlasting" (Ps. 139:23–24).

While there is no one right way to engage in healthy self-reflection, it will surely include some combination of the following practices:

- Stopping—having the brave willingness to detach from a frantic world for a time in order to take an unflinching look at your heart and life
- Solitude—getting alone
- Silence—being quiet and still
- Prayer—talking at length with God
- Bible reading—listening to God speak in his Word

◉ Community—seeking insight from a small circle of people you trust

◉ Journaling—honestly expressing thoughts, feelings, questions, concerns, hang-ups, hurts, prayers, etc. on paper or a computer screen, perhaps in a password-protected file

All of these activities, over time, increase personal awareness, and can lead to greater objectivity and a healthier perspective.

## Feedback from Others

"I love getting feedback!" one of our seminar promoters exclaimed one day. His comment caught me by surprise. Most people I know are hesitant to receive feedback. They wince or cringe at the suggestion. Others avoid it like the proverbial plague. No doubt, past reminders of harsh criticism still haunt them. They carry the scars of hurtful words. Yet when we resist feedback, we deprive ourselves of wisdom and insight that could really help us. Psalm 141:5 says, "Let a righteous man strike me—that is a kindness; let him rebuke me—that is oil on my head. My head will not refuse it."

My promoter friend wasn't kidding. Not only is he a glad recipient of feedback, I can testify that he is great at giving feedback. After my presentation, he started with affirmation:

..............................................................

That was great! The pastors were really engaged. Even though it took longer, I think it was wise that you gave us extra time to continue our discussions with each other about our difficult ministry situations. However, the other exercise you started but didn't finish (or process with us) left me feeling frustrated. I understand how it happened. I've done the same thing myself before. But in my opinion, it's better not to start an exercise if you don't have ample time to finish it and process it together. All in all, I am so excited that our pastors had this opportunity for training!

................................................................

Wow! Perfect. His feedback after a presentation left me feeling affirmed. And it prepared me for an even better presentation next time.

That's what honest feedback from others does. It gives us the much-needed opportunity to see ourselves from another's perspective. Feedback reveals our blind spots. It makes us more effective in our ministries and interpersonal interactions. The breakfast of champions, feedback is invaluable.

I'll grant you that most people are not as adept at giving feedback as the leader above was for me. Nevertheless, feedback—whether it's given skillfully or clumsily, solicited or unsolicited, delivered tactfully or harshly—is a gift. It allows us to see ourselves or our efforts through the eyes of another. In the words of wise King Solomon: "Better is open rebuke than hidden love. Wounds from a friend can be trusted, but an enemy multiplies kisses" (Prov. 27:5–6).

## Why Does Personal Insight Matter?

Personal insight is important for a number of reasons. Let me list just four reasons why you need to make it a priority:

### Personal Insight Is Required by Scripture

The Bible places enormous value on personal insight. *The Message* paraphrase of Proverbs 4:23 reads: "Keep vigilant watch over your heart; that's where life starts." The big idea in this little verse is that we will never understand our outer actions apart from first reckoning with our inner condition. We have to constantly monitor our moods, thoughts, beliefs, attitudes, and more.

The prophets and apostles frequently urged the people of God to examine themselves (see Lam. 3:40; 1 Cor. 11:28; 2 Cor. 13:5). Jesus warned about the normal human tendency to see faults in others, but not in ourselves, prompting that famous command to remove the "plank" from one's own eye before trying to remove "the speck of sawdust" from the eye of another (see Luke 6:41–42).

## Personal Insight Is a Top Predictor of Leadership Success

In an article entitled "Nice Guys Finish First," the American Management Association reported on research from Cornell University that found self-awareness to be the number one predictor of leadership success.[1] We shouldn't be surprised. Great leaders throughout history have always espoused the value of personal insight.

- Benjamin Franklin said, "Observe all men; thyself most."[2]
- Psychologist Carl Jung noted, "Until you make the unconscious conscious, it will direct your life and you will call it fate."[3]
- Sun Tzu, ancient Chinese general and philosopher credited with writing the famous military book entitled *The Art of War*, warned, "If you know the enemy and know yourself, you need not fear the result of a hundred battles. If you know yourself but not the enemy, for every victory gained you will also suffer a defeat. If you know neither the enemy nor yourself, you will succumb in every battle."[4]
- Psychologist Abraham Maslow concluded, "Whereas the average individuals often have not the slightest idea of what they are, of what they want, of what their own opinions are, self-actualizing individuals have superior awareness of their own impulses, desires, opinions, and subjective reactions in general."[5]

## Personal Insight Is a Prerequisite to Growth and Change

A third reason personal insight matters is that growth and change are impossible without it. How can we change what we don't know needs changing? Why would we attempt to fix something that we're not even aware is broken? Learning the truth about yourself can be shocking and sobering. Think about going to the doctor, visiting your financial planner, or taking the car in to discover the source of that awful grinding noise. Sometimes the truth is painful or scary. But apart from the truth we'd never take a step in a new and better direction.

The old saying is true: Knowledge really *is* power. It enables us to direct our energies toward addressing problems. Becoming aware of our internal condition and emotional ups and downs puts us in position to manage those emotions and express them in healthy and constructive ways. By contrast, being unaware of our emotions leaves us at their mercy. They dominate us and lead us around. When we don't know why we do things, we're naturally more inclined to repeat patterns that are unhelpful, self-sabotaging, or that impede our relationships. Personal insight allows us to do a self-check on our moods and motives, paving the way for us to make adjustments.

Personally, I've noticed I have a tendency to push too hard without taking a break. Then I start stressing over minor issues. So now, when I notice myself feeling especially tired in the afternoon or obsessing over questions like "Did I turn off the stove?" I realize that these are indicators that I need to stop and rest. You may not find yourself acting as neurotic as that! However, do you ever notice yourself becoming more impatient, irritable, overeating, or not sleeping well? You may need to take a closer look at the causes. When you do, you will likely find opportunities for growth and change.

Self-monitoring is what enables us to take proactive steps. Because he is a competent get-it-done type leader, Pastor Jim is learning that he quickly gets frustrated when members of his church don't want to move as quickly as he'd like. Staying consciously aware of this tendency enables Jim to guard his attitude (and his tongue!) in board meetings. Such self-knowledge is crucial when negative emotions like stress, anxiety, or resentment rise up within us.

## Personal Insight Is Foundational to Understanding and Relating to Others

How can you and I hope to understand others and know how to engage with them if we don't first have some understanding of ourselves? How can we empathize with what others are feeling or sense what they need if we don't have a clue about our own feelings and needs?

Personal insight lays the foundation for the other three components of emotional intelligence: personal mastery, relational insight, and relational mastery. You can't manage yourself, interact effectively with others, or understand the feelings, needs, and perspectives of those you are trying to lead without a foundation of personal insight. Understanding what someone else is feeling in a particular situation requires empathy and compassion. Howard Hendricks put it this way: "You cannot impart what you do not possess." [6] In other words, it takes a pastor with personal insight to help others develop personal insight.

Even though he is right on the edge of burnout, Pastor Bill feels hopeful. Thanks to epiphanies big and small (for example, church happenings, his weary heart), mixed with assorted "aha" moments (for example, brave feedback from a sweet wife, informal conversations, and formal presentations at a timely pastors' conference), Bill is seeing some very important (though not very flattering) truths about himself:

- He's definitely a people pleaser.
- The quintessential nice guy, he has a hard time saying no.
- He doesn't have any replenishing hobbies.
- He works too much and rests too little.

Bill is hopeful because of the gospel. He can change by the power of God. He doesn't have to keep going like this.

To summarize, when it comes to personal insight:

- We all have *some* self-awareness. Let's put to death the idea that this is a capacity that only a few elite leaders possess.
- We all have blind spots. That's not a criticism; it's a statement of fact. Healthy leaders don't deny this reality, nor do they look at their various shortcomings and flaws and throw up their hands. Instead, they own their blind spots and go to work trying to identify and correct misguided ways of thinking and interacting.
- We can grow and change. We really can develop further personal insight. In fact, as a psychologist, I help people grow their personal insight every day.
- Developing personal insight will enhance our ministries as well as our personal lives and interpersonal relationships.

### Four Skills and Habits of Personal Insight

Now that we have defined personal insight and described why it's so essential, let's consider how to develop it.

I have identified four skills that help people gain personal insight. To be an emotionally intelligent leader, you will need to learn and practice these four skills. If you do that, these practices will become habits. When that happens, you'll be a much healthier leader—a person with rare personal insight.

## Skill 1: Monitoring Your Emotions

The first skill in gaining personal insight is monitoring one's emotions. Or, we could say, keeping tabs on the emotional currents ebbing and flowing inside of us.

### Bill's Experience

Leading up to the pastors' conference, Bill was coming to terms with the fact that he could no longer ignore his weariness and apathy. People—not just Celeste—had started to notice that he seemed down.

The conversations with Susan and Jim, and the content of the plenary and workshop sessions, only served to confirm this. Bill was ready to get to the bottom of what was taking place in his soul. At breakfast on the final day of the conference, Jim had made an offhanded comment about how suppressing anger can sometimes lead to depression. All the way home, Bill pondered that thought. He didn't think of himself as an angry guy. But was he?

Bill began praying about that idea—and journaling. As he did, all sorts of emotions came bubbling to the surface. One day it finally dawned on him that he *was* angry about some things—not anyone in particular, but at himself. He was angry at the way he let the church completely dictate his schedule, angry at the way he often bit his tongue for fear of saying something true that would upset others, and angry that he had stopped pursuing his beloved hobby of fishing because of the "jokey" criticism he heard early on in ministry whenever he took off and went to the lake. Journaling led to other epiphanies such as how much he was always afraid of displeasing others. Bill was stunned. He hadn't realized how much these powerful feelings—fear and anger—had been swirling around in his heart and ministry.

This prompted Bill to pay more attention, Proverbs 4:23–style. He began consciously identifying what he was feeling in any given moment:

insecure, envious, anxious, critical, glad. Just having this awareness was immensely helpful. It enabled Bill to then ask questions like, "Why am I feeling this way? What triggered these feelings? What are my tendencies when I feel this way? What precautions do I need to take?" And most importantly, "What's true in this situation?"

Imagine if Bill had been more in tune with his own feelings early on in his ministry. Could he have avoided getting to his current level of discouragement and burnout? Only God can say. Nevertheless, as previously stated, Bill left the conference hopeful. The things he learned there are helping him gain the skill of personal insight. He has begun to make changes that will reinvigorate him and help him thrive in ministry long-term.

## My Experience

It was my own personal therapy and my counseling training years ago that helped me see a truth I had never realized: My regular vocabulary included very few, if any, *feeling* words. I had very little personal insight into the state of my heart. I'm sure this was largely due to the fact that I grew up in a stoic family where feelings were not discussed.

When I was eight, my brother Steve served a year in Vietnam as an infantryman. Every night my family would gather around the TV set to watch CBS anchorman Walter Cronkite share the latest news from Southeast Asia: how many American soldiers were missing, wounded, or dead. When the broadcast ended each evening, everyone in my family stood up and left the living room—without saying a word. We just went about our individual activities. But no one dared bring up what we had just heard. No one talked about the fear that filled our home and permeated our hearts. Conversation was limited to lighter, more superficial topics. Can you imagine the anxiety and dread my parents must have felt? Or the terror I experienced in my own eight-year-old heart? Indeed, it was so bad that my mother had to take me to the doctor for stomach problems that year!

I don't know why my family was like that. But I do know that the way our family of origin deals with feelings is our first and perhaps biggest influence on how we will deal with feelings. Now you can see why as an adult I had to learn how to be aware of my emotions, how to talk about them, and then how to deal with them. But look at it this way: The girl who grew up in a stoic family is now writing a book about emotions and their impact on people. If I can learn this skill, you surely can!

Just like Bill, journaling helped me get more in touch with my feelings. I'm glad to be able to say that through practice, the skill of monitoring my feelings has since become an unconscious, automatic habit. Today I am able to name what's really going on inside me. This helps me monitor my stress and avoid burnout. More importantly, it helps me maintain the optimism, gratitude, and personal energy I need to accomplish my goals.

I can hear the protests of some readers: "Please! Give me a break! All this touchy-feely junk, all this emphasis on emotions is silly, even dangerous. Emotions are notoriously unreliable! You can't trust your feelings! In fact, most times, you should ignore them!"

Hear me out: I'm not advocating that we let our emotions run our lives. That would be disastrous! I am saying that emotions are important—and that we should pay close attention to them. Someone has wisely said that we should think of feelings as functioning like the assorted gauges on an automobile dashboard. Those lighted symbols don't make the car go. They serve only to indicate and warn. Their purpose is to let us know when it's time to pull over, find a garage, and raise the hood. That's one very important function of emotions—they're like warning lights on the dashboards of our lives.

Emotions provide us with information and help us react. Take fear, for example. It serves to keep us from doing dangerous things and it also prompts us to seek safety. What about anger? It's what we instinctively feel when we perceive an injustice. Anger provides us with the energy needed to take action.

Physiologically, those strong feelings of anger and fear work this way. They send signals to our bodies that it's time to produce adrenaline. In the cascade of stress hormones that get released, our heart rates increase, our pupils dilate, and our breathing intensifies. In short, the emotion regulation centers of our brain go on high alert. At the same time, the higher order reasoning and problem-solving portions of our brain become less active. Instantly we are amped up to meet whatever challenge we are facing: anger fuels us for fighting; fear fuels us to flee.

If all that biology is lost on you, don't worry. You don't have to become an endocrinologist to gain personal insight into your feelings. But you do need to get better at tuning in to all the emotions that constantly rise and fall in your heart. You need to develop the ability to correctly name whatever it is you're feeling: threatened, resentful, jealous, guilty, embarrassed, ashamed, or something else. Because unless and until you diagnose exactly what you are feeling, you can't reflect prayerfully on your situation and figure out what's needed. In naming your feelings, you may come to see that they are rooted in reality and are calling for action. Or you may realize your feelings are simply rooted in wrong thoughts and beliefs.

## Five Basic Emotions

Emotions are like colors. The five primary emotions are fear, anger, sadness, happiness, and surprise. Other common feelings are shades or blends of these basic emotions. Shades of anger include irritability, frustration, rage, and others. Shades of sadness: despondence, depression, disappointment.

Naming our emotions paves the way for us to manage them in a healthy, God-honoring way. In addition, it enhances our ability to connect emotionally with others and tune in to what they may be feeling.

# Emotions Vocabulary List

| Intensity | Happy | Sad | | Angry | | Scared | Confus |
|---|---|---|---|---|---|---|---|
| **Strong** | ecstatic<br>elated<br>energized<br>enthusiastic<br>excited<br>exuberant<br>jubilant<br>loved<br>marvelous<br>terrific<br>thrilled<br>uplifted | crushed<br>defeated<br>dejected<br>depressed<br>devastated<br>disgraced<br>drained<br>exhausted<br>helpless<br>hopeless<br>hurt<br>rejected<br>terrible<br>unloved<br>unwanted<br>discarded | sorrowful<br>uncared for<br>worthless<br>wounded<br>burdened<br>condemned<br>demoralized<br>deserted<br>distraught<br>empty<br>grievous<br>humbled<br>miserable<br>mournful<br>pitiful | abused<br>betrayed<br>enraged<br>furious<br>hateful<br>hostile<br>humiliated<br>incensed<br>outraged<br>pissed off<br>rebellious<br>repulsed<br>seething<br>strangled<br>vengeful | exploited<br>fuming<br>mad<br>patronized<br>repulsed<br>spiteful<br>throttled<br>used<br>vindictive | afraid<br>appalled<br>desperate<br>dread<br>fearful<br>frantic<br>horrified<br>intimidated<br>overwhelmed<br>panicky<br>petrified<br>shocked<br>terrified<br>tormented<br>vulnerable | baffled<br>bewilder<br>constrict<br>direction<br>flustered<br>stagnant<br>trapped |
| **Mild** | admired<br>alive<br>amused<br>appreciated<br>assured<br>cheerful<br>confident<br>delighted<br>determined<br>encouraged<br>fulfilled<br>grateful<br>gratified<br>joyful<br>justified<br>optimistic<br>proud<br>relieved<br>resolved<br>respected<br>valued | ashamed<br>despised<br>disappointed<br>discouraged<br>disheartened<br>disillusioned<br>dismal<br>distant<br>distressed<br>inadequate<br>isolated<br>lonely<br>neglected<br>slighted | unappreciated<br>upset<br>abandoned<br>alienated<br>degraded<br>deprived<br>disturbed<br>drained<br>islanded<br>resigned<br>slighted<br>wasted | agitated<br>annoyed<br>controlled<br>disgusted<br>exasperated<br>frustrated<br>harassed<br>infantilized<br>irritated<br>offended<br>peeved<br>resentful<br>ridiculed<br>smothered<br>stifled | aggravated<br>anguished<br>cheated<br>coerced<br>deceived<br>dominated<br>provoked | alarmed<br>apprehensive<br>axed<br>defensive<br>guarded<br>insecure<br>shaken<br>skeptical<br>startled<br>stunned<br>suspicious<br>tense<br>threatened<br>uneasy | ambivale<br>awkward<br>disorgan<br>doubt<br>foggy<br>hesitant<br>misunder<br>perplexe<br>puzzled<br>torn<br>troubled |
| **Weak** | flattered<br>fortunate<br>glad<br>good<br>hopeful<br>peaceful<br>pleased<br>relaxed<br>satisfied | apathetic<br>bad<br>deflated<br>disenchanted<br>lost<br>sorry | | dismayed<br>displeased<br>tolerant<br>uptight | | anxious<br>concerned<br>doubtful<br>impatient<br>nervous<br>perplexed<br>reluctant<br>shy<br>timid<br>unsure | bothered<br>distracte<br>surprised<br>uncertai<br>uncomfo<br>undecide<br>unsettle<br>unsure |

I suggest keeping this chart handy—and referring to it often—as you read through this book. By consulting it often, you'll find yourself better able to talk about feelings, or as someone put it, "You'll become more conversant in the language of the heart."

## Common Emotional Reactions to Everyday Situations

Common emotional responses vary from person to person. An unexpected change in plans may spark disappointment, annoyance, or anxiety. An unfair situation often triggers anger or outrage. We associate loss with sadness and grief, but it often involves initial shock, anger, or even relief. Processing grief healthily eventually leads to a sense of peace.

Let's use Pastor Susan as an example for how various situations in her life have prompted assorted emotional reactions.

- When Susan thought she was pregnant only eight months into marriage, she felt a strange combination of *joy* and *anxiety*. When an EPT test and visit to her ob-gyn revealed she was *not* expecting, she felt a weird mixture of *relief* and *sadness*.
- When she got her letter of acceptance to divinity school, she felt both *excitement* and *trepidation*.
- On her last day of teaching, when her students showered her with affection, Susan felt *surprised*, *loved*, and *accepted*. But she also suddenly felt *torn*—like maybe she was making a big mistake.
- When Susan finished divinity school, she was filled with immense *joy*, *gratitude*, and *pride* ("By God's grace, I actually did it!").
- When Susan preached her first sermon to a full auditorium at her first church, she felt *hopeful* and *thrilled*, *energized* and *eager* for the challenge ahead.
- When a family left her church just months after her arrival, she felt *deflated* and *discouraged*.

⊙ A couple of subpar sermons in a row led to feelings of *embarrassment* and a nagging sense of *fear*.

⊙ A semi-contentious board meeting filled her with *uncertainty*, *self-doubt*, and *worry*.

Keep in mind that these feelings come from Susan's unique experience. Her particular emotional responses are a reflection of her one-of-a-kind values, beliefs, history, and sensitivities. Some of the things that gnaw at her would not be a blip on the radar for someone else. Each person's emotional responses are unique.

## Learning to Monitor Your Feelings

We have mentioned this already, but it's worth saying again: One way a leader can get better at identifying and monitoring his/her feelings is by **journaling**.

There really aren't any *rules* for journaling. You can go old school with pen and notebook. Or you can be high tech and create a password-protected folder/file on your computer or tablet. The point is to express your thoughts and feelings honestly.

Since the pastors' conference, Bill has been journaling for a few minutes every day. Here's a snippet:

I was encouraged for about a week after the conference. Motivated. Since then I guess I've reverted. I can't stop second-guessing myself. I'm constantly worried that I'm screwing up, that my priorities are wrong. That I should be doing something, anything, other than what I *am* doing. No confidence in any impulse I have. Every decision freezes me. Because if I choose to do "this," then I won't be doing "that" (and maybe "that" is exactly what I should be doing!). Thus, I am unable to be in the moment, enjoy it, and rest in the sure knowledge that the Good Shepherd loves me and sees me and is leading me. Sure wish I could "know" that in the depths of my being. . . .

Journal entries don't have to be a certain length. They can be one sentence: "Lord, today I feel exhausted, and I need strength." They don't even have to be written in complete sentences. Here's a journal entry from Susan:

Woke at 4:11 a.m. and couldn't go back. Nervous!!! What's eating at me?

- The upcoming visit by Mark's parents . . . ugh!
- Lord, how can we afford a new transmission?
- The weird vibe I get every time I try to talk to the Perlmans
- Way behind in my sermon prep this week—but I promised to fix chili for Mark's team on Thursday night

You can include prayers. Lists. Random thoughts. Thought-provoking quotes. Comments about Bible verses. Whatever. Nobody's grading you.

The steps—if there is such a thing in journaling—are easy. Follow the three Bs:

1. **Bring** your whole life—the good, bad, and ugly—into God's presence.
2. **Be** aware. Notice. Pay attention to what is happening inside you.
3. **Be** courageous enough to be honest about what's really going on inside and out.

The Yale Center for Emotional Intelligence has developed an app that makes it easy to check in on yourself and record what you are feeling. Information and download directions are available at moodmeterapp. com/science/. You can set the program on your phone to prompt you at desired times to record your feelings. If you do this on a regular basis, you will begin to see your emotional patterns.

Other online sites offer daily mood charts you can download. Users simply record what they are feeling at various times each day and include extra notes about what circumstances are contributing to those feelings.

Are you ready to try it? Here's an activity to help you get started.

## Journaling Activity

Write down several feelings you have experienced today—or if it's early in the day, how you feel about what the day may hold. Use the feeling words chart (page 76) if you get stuck or to try out new feeling words.

Analyze and record what was happening when you felt what you felt. Try using the basic formula:

I feel/felt_____ when _____.

For example, Bill might write:

- I felt conflicted when I realized that I had a dual commitment.
- I felt worried when I realized how disappointed and upset my wife would be.
- I felt defeated, frustrated, and angry when the committee member called to criticize me for forgetting to mention the new donor.

On a better day he might write:

- ◉ I felt happy and competent at my job when Mrs. Jones expressed how much it meant for me to pray with her in the hospital.
- ◉ I felt excited when my wife said she wanted to go on a date.
- ◉ I felt hopeful when I told my board I was going to take up my hobby of fishing again, and they actually acted relieved and happy for me!

## Skill 2: Tuning In to Self-Talk

The second key skill in gaining more personal insight is asking the question, What sorts of things do I say to myself or tell myself?

Here's the truth: We all have a running narrative in our head. It's like we have a team of announcers inside the broadcast booth of our brain. One voice offers a play-by-play description of unfolding events. So, for example, Bill passes Susan on the last day of the conference, and the voice in his head notes, "There's Susan and she doesn't look happy." Suddenly, another voice provides a little color commentary, "Maybe she's offended by something you said yesterday." We're so accustomed to this self-talk that we rarely stop to consider exactly what we are saying to ourselves and the effects this inner monologue is having on us or our moods.

Sometimes self-talk serves to help us. We might remind ourselves not to forget to call a parishioner who was supposed to get test results this afternoon. Or we might reflect internally on an external situation ("Susan looks unhappy"), resist wild speculations ("She's probably angry with me"), and instead consider options for how to respond appropriately ("At the break, I'll try to find her and see if she's okay").

But some self-talk hinders us. Chiding ourselves for past failures, having imaginary arguments with our opponents, nursing grudges, and engaging in unfounded "what if" scenarios will thwart our attempts at personal and relational mastery.

Destructive self-talk is the inner conversation that emerges from events and our misinterpretation of those events. It is less what happens to us and more how we think about those events that determines our mood and our course. We often fail to see the impact that negative self-talk is having on our feelings, actions, and overall well-being.

My work with people who are battling depression or anxiety illustrates this point. Frequently clients report to me that depression sometimes rolls over them like a cloud, causing them to feel helpless and overwhelmed. Others complain of unexpected anxiety that seemingly comes from nowhere, leaving them biting off their fingernails.

I urge such clients to keep paper and pen handy and to record the times and specific circumstances surrounding each episode of deep sadness or anxiety. What external events were unfolding? What thoughts were their minds entertaining? With a little intentionality, clients are able to use these "thought logs" to pinpoint certain situations, unhealthy patterns of thinking, or wrong beliefs behind destructive self-talk.

Examples of negative or anxiety-producing thoughts include "I can't" or "I must" or "I should." Saying "I can't" generally leads to feelings of powerlessness or discouragement, while saying "I must" or "I should" creates overwhelming expectations that typically result in anxiety, stress, disappointment, and self-loathing.

Examples of anger-producing thoughts often start with phrases such as, "He/she should" or "They never." This is where you create agendas for people around you and then invoice them whenever they fail to live up to your demands. Such ways of thinking invariably lead to frustration, resentment, and bitterness.

When Pastor Bill's council member called him and reamed him out for failing to recognize a new donor, the subconscious voice in Bill's head started in: *No matter what I do I can never please these people! Some leader I am. I can't do anything right. I always screw up.*

No wonder he felt deflated and angry—at both himself and "these people." The feelings came so quickly he didn't realize that his own thoughts about being chided were as responsible for his bad feelings as the criticism itself!

Do you see how our thoughts and beliefs (revealed in our self-talk) drive our feelings? Do you see how such thinking would naturally lead anyone to frustration, anger, and a sense of failure and resignation? Do you see how tuning in to our self-talk can help us gain greater insight into our deepest needs, fears, motivations, and beliefs?

Being mindful of self-talk helps us analyze whether the things we are saying to ourselves are helping or hindering us. We'll address this at more length in the next chapter.

### What Is Mind-Set?

Mind-set is the sum total of all your self-talk. Put all your interior conversations together, and an overall picture will come into view—a picture of how you see yourself, look at others, and view circumstances. *Mind-set* is another word for perspective. It's your mental grid, your big view of the world.

It's important to realize that we don't only have individual thoughts, but we have *patterns of thinking* that shape and form our views about life. Our mind-set, like the rudder on a ship, continually steers us in a certain direction in life. No wonder Proverbs 23:7 says that as a man "thinketh in his heart, so is he" (KJV). More than any other factor, our mind-set determines our life experience.

So how do we know what our mind-set is? Easy. Just listen to your everyday self-talk. Perk up your ears! If you tune in to the voice in your head, you'll learn volumes about yourself—where your identity lies, what your motivations are, where you find significance, how you view yourself, how you think of others, whether you are naturally optimistic or pessimistic, and so much more.

Remember Pastor Bill's self-talk? *No matter what I do I can never please these people! Some leader I am. I can't do anything right. I always screw up.* In and behind these words, we hear a hunger to please, a desire for the approval of others. We hear feelings of inadequacy, and a lack of confidence. Nobody wants to be rejected, but perhaps this fear drives Bill more than he realizes.

That's what analyzing our self-talk can do for us. It can give us an unfiltered, unedited peek at our hurts and hang-ups, our insecurities and internal beliefs that contribute to our overall perspective. The way we see ourselves and others is generally deep-seated. We can trace many of our typical responses back to childhood events and the conclusions we drew from those events. We often take our cues from our previous interactions with others—parents, siblings, teachers, classmates, and friends.

Unconsciously, as children, we were forming our sense of identity and worth and purpose. Maybe at church you heard you were loved unconditionally by a gracious and good God. But at home, acceptance was based solely on your ability to please your parents. Meanwhile at school you learned that your worth was tied to how well you could read and add and spell and throw a ball. A twisted message emerged: *Please others and perform flawlessly, and life will go well for you!* Think of how many kids bring such baggage into adulthood—and into pastoral ministry.

One such kid becomes a pastor who is an approval addict. He tries to please everyone. Or she becomes a perfectionist who is never satisfied. Nothing ever measures up. Ten people can rave about her sermon, but she obsesses over the one stinging comment sent by an anonymous person in an email.

This is why you need to pay attention to self-talk. Because when you connect your identity and self-worth to whether you please everyone and perform flawlessly, you can be sure certain things are ahead:

- ◉ It will be harder to relax and just be yourself.
- ◉ It will be harder to be open, authentic, and admit mistakes.
- ◉ You will become defensive at the slightest hint of criticism.
- ◉ You will overwork to prove yourself, and you won't recognize when you need a break.
- ◉ You will worry too much and work too hard at winning favor and trying to make people like you.
- ◉ Depression and burnout will start circling overhead like vultures.

Bill is exhibit A of this. I'm not speaking ill of him. He is a good and faithful pastor. He genuinely loves the people in his flock, and they can tell. Most respond warmly to his ministry. He's a humble guy with a mostly positive mind-set. He's not jealous of the blessings or abilities of others. He sees people with compassion and kindness, giving grace to failures.

Yet Bill can sometimes fall into old ways of thinking. This tends to happen after a negative event—like when someone criticizes him or an event goes badly. Suddenly Bill views himself as a failure. When operating under that mind-set, the guy who has grace for everyone else doesn't give much grace to himself. On the contrary, he becomes self-critical, which makes him feel increasingly insecure, which creates within himself a heightened desire for others' approval in order to prop himself up!

What a vicious cycle. When he doesn't get affirmation, Bill sometimes slips into mild depression. This leads to a loss of energy, motivation, passion, and vision. Sadly, I bet you know someone like Bill.

Let's do some soul work. Here's another activity to help you grow in personal insight, particularly in the area understanding your overall mind-set.

## Identity Checklist Activity

Ponder the following list. Place a check mark beside the items that are true of you.

\_\_\_\_ I feel an overwhelming need to please others.

\_\_\_\_ I have an inordinate desire to be in control.

\_\_\_\_ I need to be needed.

\_\_\_\_ I always feel like I have to prove myself.

\_\_\_\_ I crave attention (in other words, being in the limelight).

\_\_\_\_ I feel suffocated when I don't get recognition, compliments, affirmation.

\_\_\_\_ I have a powerful need to be right.

\_\_\_\_ I'm extremely competitive; losing feels like death.

\_\_\_\_ I am driven by a fear of failure.

\_\_\_\_ I'm deathly afraid of rejection.

\_\_\_\_ I have an inordinate fear of being taken advantage of.

\_\_\_\_ I have an excessive fear of losing control.

\_\_\_\_ I'll do anything to avoid looking foolish.

Set aside a time to self-reflect through journaling, prayer, or talking with someone about the items you checked.

## Skill 3: Identifying Triggers

The third habit in gaining personal insight is being able to identify and recognize your hot buttons—the situations that are likely to trigger an impulsive (and often destructive) reaction.

Remember when Pastor Jim told Susan and Bill that he has always tended to have a knee-jerk reaction to criticism and that this tendency had gotten him into trouble more than once? It's true. Jim's outbursts always shocked and perplexed others the first time they encountered them. A few more aggressive types went toe-to-toe with Jim. But generally, both in business and ministry, most colleagues and board members wilted. They refrained from challenging Jim or his ideas. They learned that offering even loving, constructive feedback would trigger his displeasure, so they stopped doing it.

Jim didn't reveal the fact that his wife recently complained that he doesn't care about her or her feelings, or that he bristled when she said it. This made no sense to him. He thought it should be obvious that he cares! Everywhere he goes—business, church, home—Jim feels like people are taking shots at him.

Why is Jim so sensitive, so defensive about criticism—even from his loving wife and loyal board members? It's probably because when he was younger Jim's father criticized him constantly. He was that dad who pointed out every missed play on the soccer field; who asked why Jim had only made a 98 on a test and not a perfect score; who blew his stack when Jim slightly scratched the bumper on the family's new station wagon; and who shook his head in embarrassment when Jim forgot his lines in the school play.

Is it any wonder, then, that Jim frequently felt demoralized, worthless, and angry? Or that he responded by trying feverishly to avoid screwing up—and frantically scrambling to cover up any real or perceived mistakes?

As an adult, Pastor Jim gets testy even when people offer innocent suggestions for how things might be done better—and he gets really triggered if anyone outright criticizes him. Feeling attacked and shamed, vulnerable and insecure, all Jim's fight or flight mechanisms kick in. Immediately he goes into self-protection mode—defending himself and trying to prove that he is correct. He will get snarky and verbally vicious if that's what it takes to ward off his "attacker." None of this is objective, rational, or preconceived. It is subconscious and instant. Remember the board meeting in which he encountered resistance? He fought (saying things he shouldn't have said), and then he fled (storming out of the room).

## Identify Knee-Jerk Reactions

The phrase *emotionally triggered* typically refers to excessive, over-the-top, or out-of-context emotional reactions. Because most of us have painful events in our past that we haven't fully processed in a healthy way, we are highly sensitive to certain situations, topics, or words that resurrect those memories. For example, let's say your mom constantly nagged you about overeating. Chances are good you will be triggered if a friend innocently says, "I know how much you love this—that's why I doubled the recipe."

Ocean rip currents are dangerous for a couple of reasons: one, they're not easy to recognize; and two, they can take people far from shore in a hurry. Emotional rip currents are similar. They arise suddenly from whatever default defense mechanisms we have developed, and they can take us places we never intended or wanted to go. Under their power, we do and say things we never meant to say. In the grips of powerful emotions of fear, anger, or depression, we often react (rather than respond) in a reflexive way, rather than from a place of thoughtful reflection.

Facing criticism, Jim blew up in a fit of anger. Bill withered in defeat. This is typical. Some people shut down when emotionally triggered. Others power up. Still others are overwhelmed with anxiety or panic. These powerful emotions surge up and out from deep within our souls. They are unexpected. They catch us off guard. Depending on the feeling, our default defense mechanisms kick in. If it's shame, we try to hide; anger, we lash out; panic, we freeze; fear, we fight or flee.

Thus it's extremely helpful to identify the sort of events and situations that trigger strong emotion. Then we need to gain insight into the history behind those feelings. Such awareness gives us the ability, with God's help, to have a better response.

So why don't more people take the time to try to understand their trigger points? Probably because it's not fun to revisit painful moments from our past or to sort through unpleasant feelings. The process feels counterintuitive: reliving pain to relieve pain. Yet analyzing and gaining insight into these triggers allows us to gain control over them rather than merely suppress, deny, or give in to them.

## Know Your Hot Buttons Tool

Here's an activity that can help you identify your emotional triggers or hot buttons.

Think of a recent incident in which your emotional reaction was disproportionate or out of context. In short, you overreacted, sobbed uncontrollably, blew up, or suddenly felt out of sorts at what should have been a happy event.

Describe the situation itself.

Describe what you felt during the situation as best as you can recall.

Describe your reaction (in other words, what you felt, said, or did).

Describe your thoughts at that time.

Consider these deeper reflection questions:

- When have you felt this way before?
- When have you previously reacted this way?
- Do you recall ever feeling like this in childhood? If so, describe the childhood event and your feelings.
- What does your reaction suggest about your underlying values, beliefs, or mind-set?
- Was this reaction an anomaly or is this a recurring pattern in your life?

## Skill 4: Asking for Feedback

A fourth practice that is common among leaders with a healthy level of personal insight is *seeking feedback*. Unless you are a mind reader, you can't possibly know how you come across to others. Without feedback, you can't be sure if your impact is positive or negative. Wise leaders, therefore, solicit regular and comprehensive input. Leaders who are not open to feedback often experience "wrecks" for the same reason that many drivers have accidents—their blind spots keep them from seeing danger.

Feedback, especially unsolicited feedback, can be difficult to hear. Nevertheless, feedback, even when it's critical, is a gift. No wonder Scripture admonishes us to hear feedback. "Fools think their own way is right, but the wise listen to others" (Prov. 12:15 NLT).

I know what you may be thinking: *That all sounds noble and good, but I'm terrified of what people might tell me if I ask them to be honest with me!*

Believe me, I hear you! It's painful to hear all the ways that you've disappointed others and failed to measure up. But this is what makes the gospel so beautiful, powerful, and breathtaking. Properly understood, the good news of Jesus frees us from the crippling fear of criticism. How so? Because the gospel is the ultimate feedback: unflinching truth and absolute grace. The gospel says we are terribly flawed—every single one of us. In other words, someone telling us we screwed up isn't really "news." At the same time, the gospel declares that we are fiercely and perfectly loved—even in our worst failure! And it further says that God is committed to making us like his Son. The work he has begun in us, he *will* complete (see Phil. 1:6). So, we can relax. We don't have to pretend we're better than we are. Since we are all in process, the pressure's off. None of us has it all together. We are all works in progress, and we're called to help each other make progress in the faith. Feedback is our friend, not our enemy.

## Examples of Formal Feedback

Here are some types of opportunities to hear formal feedback from others:

- Leadership assessments
- Emotional Intelligence assessments
- 360 Assessments (assessment information gathered from others who know you)
- Feedback from a coach, mentor, or therapist
- Honest conversations with those who know you best and love you most

## Examples of Informal Feedback

Here are some ways in which you might receive informal feedback:

- Unsolicited feedback. This could include casual comments from others made in passing.
- Direct criticism. Humble leaders whose hope is solely in the gospel can prayerfully consider even harsh attacks, asking, "Lord, is there any truth to this? What, if anything, do I need to see in this?"
- Solicited feedback in an informal manner. This can be as simple as asking others what they think about certain aspects of your leadership. For example, you might ask, "Hey, how did I come across to you when the Millers started asking questions about cost of the new building?

Being open to and desiring feedback helps create a culture of transparency. If people think that you are not truly receptive to feedback, they generally won't give it—or at least not until they are upset. Even when we are open to feedback, however, many still resist providing anything more than "Wonderful message today, Pastor!"

## *Emotional Intelligence Begins with Personal Insight*

If you want to be an effective leader—especially a pastoral leader—you have to develop personal insight. This component of emotional intelligence helps us avoid being dominated by negative, unhealthy emotions that can damage our relationships. Personal insight shows us our blind spots and helps us grow in integrity and personal security. Ultimately, having more accurate self-knowledge will change how we relate to others and how they respond to us.

People without personal insight are stuck! They tend to repeat patterns of dysfunctional behavior. Professionally, they languish in the doldrums of stagnation. Perhaps you've met people like this. Some are prickly or moody, and others walk on eggshells around them, so as not to trigger any awkward outbursts. Personally, I find that thought both sad and scary.

All personal growth, even spiritual growth, begins with insight. In truth, that is the basic meaning of the biblical word *repentance*. It means to change one's mind and direction because of new spiritual understanding. For example, you may realize a not-so-flattering truth about yourself, and as a result you make needed changes. The insight is the prerequisite to growth. The fact that you are reading this sentence likely demonstrates your strong desire for insight and growth.

Being a Christian leader means first of all to be a follower or disciple of Christ. A disciple is a learner or student, one who is in a state of continual growth and development. He or she follows Jesus in order to become like Jesus. So my challenge to you is this: Don't simply read about emotional intelligence. Read about it, put this book down, and then embark on the hard but worthwhile journey of gaining personal insight.

# Learning Personal Mastery

Pastor Jim is known for being a strong communicator and bold leader. Because he is able to cast a clear, compelling vision, he typically generates excitement in those he leads. Consider his background in business and the church. Is it surprising that he has led a thriving business and a vibrant and growing church? Not at all. He knows how to motivate people to tackle worthy projects and get things done.

PERSONAL MASTERY

Emotionally *Intelligent*

PASTOR

*Engage, Inspire, Transform*

But being this kind of driven, task-oriented, missional leader, Jim can also get frustrated when people or events block his initiatives and goals. In those situations, if Jim is not being oh-so-careful (translation: walking in the power of the Holy Spirit), he can lash out at others. And that habit is a great *demotivator* to his board, staff, and volunteers! Most of the time Jim takes frustrations in stride, but every once in a while, his emotions get the better of him—meaning his people get the worst of him!

Meanwhile, Pastor Bill is known for being a great shepherd. He is attentive to their needs and kind in his pastoral care. Furthermore, he's a calming presence with a great reputation in the community. So what's his struggle? Likable, easygoing Bill has cultivated the habit of engaging in and listening to negative, critical self-talk which often sends him tumbling into depression.

Here's the truth: for much of his life, Bill has battled insecurity. That's not unusual in and of itself. Everybody has self-doubts—some people all the time, all people some of the time. Bill's problem is that he consistently looks outward instead of upward to shore up his sagging sense of worth and adequacy. Unconsciously, and unfortunately, he has come to seek the approval of others as the antidote to his insecurity.

When people make positive comments about his preaching, or about how things are going at the church, Bill's mood is pretty good. But let criticism come, and the voices in Bill's head turn dark. Suddenly, his insecurity spikes, and before you know it, he's in the proverbial tank. And, because he's so averse to displeasing people and losing their approval, it's difficult for Bill to have tough conversations with others. He has a tendency to duck conversations in which he fears he might be criticized. He finds it difficult to say hard but necessary things. He's cryptic and indirect, obtuse and passive in communication.

As long as everyone is happy with Bill's performance, things *seem* to work okay. But who can keep everyone happy forever? Given these factors, are you surprised that Bill feels so weary?

Imagine how much more effective Bill could be if he could squelch the critical self-talk within and master this powerful, unhealthy desire for approval. Imagine how much more effective Jim could be if he weren't so susceptible to angry outbursts and snarky comments when others seem to challenge him.

## What Is Personal Mastery?

The word *mastery* means control, so *personal mastery* in simplest terms means self-control. The apostle Paul declared that this trait or virtue of self-control is one result of being indwelt and empowered by the Holy Spirit of God (see Gal. 5:22–23). And Jesus told his followers, "Apart from me you can do nothing" (John 15:5). This sweeping statement includes exhibiting self-control. The biblical teaching is clear: We cannot manage and regulate our inward emotions and outward actions without divine enablement.

## What's the Difference between Personal Insight and Personal Mastery?

We could describe the difference in various ways:

◉ Personal insight reveals our strengths and where exactly we need to grow. Personal mastery entails actually working on personal growth areas—taking the insight we've gained and doing something with it.

◉ Personal insight is taking stock of what's true in your life (thoughts, values, behaviors, habits). Personal mastery is taking control of those things (eliminating negative thinking and bad habits, and creating new, healthy habits).

◉ Personal insight is noticing, analyzing, assessing. Personal mastery is acting, implementing, making changes.

## Two Aspects of Personal Mastery

Personal mastery entails regulating your life in two primary ways: internally, through managing your thoughts and emotions; and externally, through managing your speech and actions.

*Internal Regulation.* Emotionally intelligent pastors regulate their emotions. They don't suppress or surrender to them.

When you suppress or deny an emotion, what happens? The feeling doesn't magically disappear; you merely shove it down into your psyche where it often morphs and metastasizes!

Alternately, what happens when you surrender to an emotion? You say or do things with no filter or little thought. You react instead of respond.

The result is words and deeds that are reflexive and embarrassing—not reflective and encouraging. Sadly, we can't un-say a sentence, and life doesn't come with a button that allows us to delete our actions.

Neither option—suppressing emotions or surrendering to them—is emotional intelligence. That's the antithesis of personal mastery. Personal mastery means we are not at the mercy of our feelings. We don't have to run from them, and we don't have to give in to them. The essential concept here is that we are capable of altering and controlling our emotions!

Here's an example: On his way home from the airport, Pastor Jim was feeling pretty good. He had old Eagles tunes blaring on his car stereo and he was singing along at the top of his lungs. He was so glad he went to the conference. It had been a delightful break from his routine. His interactions with Bill, Susan, and some other pastors had been way more encouraging than he expected. And the content—all the material on emotional intelligence—was eye-opening and fascinating. He was motivated to ponder those ideas and concepts in more depth.

Just then his smartphone buzzed. Glancing down he saw a text from Greg, the board member with whom he'd had tension and disagreement recently. The message was terse: "Can you meet me tomorrow morning at 6?"

Suddenly, Jim's good mood was out the window. Instantly, he felt his heart start beating faster, his body tense up. Without even trying, his mind began to race with possible scenarios—*What does he want to talk about? The morning after I get back?* As Jim pre-lived his meeting with Greg, from deep within, a faint anger began to rise. *If he starts in about . . . then I'm going to . . . .* In no time at all, Jim was having a knock-down, drag-out argument with Greg—in his head!

Isn't it amazing how quickly our moods can change? We can go from laid back to ramped up in seconds.

But then something amazing happened. Jim caught himself.

*Wait, what am I doing? I'm having an imaginary argument based on hypothetical speculation! I'm jumping to wild conclusions with no facts whatsoever. This isn't emotionally intelligent! The truth is, I have no idea what Greg wants. It might even be positive.* Suddenly Jim began thinking about other, more edifying possibilities, and within a few minutes, he was calm again.

This, in a nutshell, is what emotionally intelligent leaders do. Rather than ignoring feelings, rather than letting their emotions run wild, carrying them away like a raging river, they acknowledge and address them. That involves thinking. That is, EI-savvy leaders analyze their feelings to see what thoughts gave rise to their troubling emotions. Where appropriate, they change their thoughts.

As Jim followed this process, he had a mini-epiphany. He was feeling worked up because he was entertaining—and blindly accepting—a bunch of unproven ideas, thoughts like: *Greg's up to no good. He's got it in for me. In our text exchange, he said things were fine between us— obviously they're not. Great! No telling what mischief he's been up to with the board while I've been gone. Obviously, he's been waiting for me to get back from this conference just so he can go off on me again. . . .*

Do you see how the thoughts we dwell on directly affect what and how we feel? Given the kinds of thoughts Jim was entertaining, is it any wonder he was feeling tense, touchy, and ready for a fight? Bonus question: What are the odds of a leader with such a mind-set having a productive meeting?

Emotionally intelligent leaders are marked by personal mastery. They monitor their mind-set. They listen to their self-talk. They then ask the question, "What's true here? Are my thoughts here aligned with reality?" Employing this little habit, EI-savvy leaders are able to make needed changes in their thinking. As a result, their emotions begin to change, too. This in turn paves the way for them to be calmer and more proficient in direct, yet nonaggressive communications with others. Their behavior is congruent with their inner state. Thus they achieve true personal mastery.

When Jim finds himself slipping into a funk, he needs to use these strategies to monitor his emotions and master his mind-set. He can learn to catch himself, remember what's true, stay positive, maintain his passion, and avoid going into shutdown mode. If he can develop these skills of personal mastery, he will be happier, more effective, and better positioned to avoid burnout.

## What Personal Mastery Looks Like

Spiritual leaders who have achieved a high degree of personal mastery manage—rather than suppress, deny, or live at the mercy of—negative emotions. This personal mastery manifests itself in four ways:

*Mastery of Mind-Set.* They consciously, regularly monitor their own self-talk and make adjustments to their thinking as necessary. They understand the effects their thoughts have on their mood and interactions and have learned to reset their mind-set when they begin to fall into negative thinking patterns.

*Mastery of Emotional Triggers.* They use their personal insight to actively work at mastering their own personal emotional triggers.

*Mastery over Communication.* They communicate directly rather than passively or aggressively.

*Mastery of Passion.* They maintain their enthusiasm for ministry by renewing themselves spiritually, emotionally, and physically. They have learned to manage stress effectively and create life balance.

In my experience, I have noticed a number of highly desirable qualities in pastors with personal mastery:

- They are better able to respond constructively to criticism.
- They are better able to bounce back from discouragement, hurtful incidents, or frustration.
- They have a more secure identity, not built on perceived success in ministry and not driven by the need to prove oneself, please others, or avoid failure.
- They develop a healthier work–life balance.

- ◉ They are better able to process anger and frustration.
- ◉ They establish healthy boundaries with the opposite sex and avoid sexual temptation.
- ◉ They manage time/scheduling and productivity better than others.

## Why Does Personal Mastery Matter?

We live in a YOLO era—**Y**ou **O**nly **L**ive **O**nce. Our culture frowns upon or mocks any kind of restraints, and instead advocates total self-indulgence and self-expression.

The Bible, meanwhile, tells believers that freedom isn't giving in to any and every whim. On the contrary, it is the ability to rein in the desires and urges that would actually enslave us and hurt others. In addition to the benefits just cited, there are other reasons personal mastery is so crucial:

*Personal Mastery Is the Mark of True Power.* It's easy to give in to raw emotion. In fact, anyone can do that (and most do). Only those with real power can resist that urge. "Better to be patient than powerful; better to have self-control than to conquer a city" (Prov. 16:32 NLT).

*Personal Mastery Can Save Us from Heartache and Danger.* Think of King David and the lifetime of heartache and headaches that flowed from his lack of personal mastery in the Bathsheba affair (see 2 Sam. 11). And before him, King Saul, who was impulsive and desperate to please people—the very opposite of personal mastery. As the book of Proverbs says, "A person without self-control is like a city with broken-down walls" (25:28 NLT).

*The Gospel Commands Personal Mastery.* Salvation does not mean we're free to live however we please. It means we have been freed to live as God intended. "For the grace of God has appeared that offers salvation to all people. It teaches us to say 'No' to ungodliness and worldly passions, and to live self-controlled, upright and godly lives in this present age" (Titus 2:11–12).

*Personal Mastery Is an Indicator of Growth.* "Indeed, we all make many mistakes. For if we could control our tongues, we would be perfect and could also control ourselves in every other way" (James 3:2 NLT).

*Personal Mastery Is the Rare Quality of Great Leaders.* Harry S. Truman once said that "in reading the lives of great men, I found that the first victory they won was over themselves . . . . Self discipline with all of them came first."[1] Stephen Covey added, "The ability to subordinate an impulse to a value is the essence of the proactive person."[2]

*Personal Mastery Builds Credibility for the Gospel and Ministry.* Why would people want to listen to us, much less follow us, if we have little control over our thoughts, words, and actions? How can we lead a board or a congregation if we can't first lead ourselves?

*Personal Mastery Enables Us to Reach Our Goals and Fulfill Our Mission.* The Olympic sprinter who succumbs to his desire for excessive sleep, fast food, and club-hopping is likely not going to be the one wearing the gold medal. The apostle Paul said as much in his letter to the Corinthian church: "Everyone who competes in the games goes into strict training. They do it to get a crown that will not last, but we do it to get a crown that will last forever" (1 Cor. 9:25).

## The Skills of Personal Mastery

Let's take a look at the skillset required for personal mastery.

## Skill 1: Resetting Your Mind-Set

If we are going to be leaders who enjoy personal mastery, we first must learn to reset our mind-set. This one ability can truly change our lives. Albert Ellis, a leading psychological theorist taught that how we think about our situations—more than the situations themselves—dictates our reality.[3]

## A Quick Mind-Set Review

As we mentioned in a prior chapter, *mind-set* refers to how we view a particular problem, person, situation, or event. More broadly speaking, mind-set is that dominant grid through which we see reality—the world, others, ourselves, and problems. We get clues to what our mind-set is by paying attention to our self-talk. Here's a quick example.

When Pastor Susan gets back from the conference, she decides to make more intentional and regular efforts to engage her congregants. She starts by showing up unannounced at the local diner on Friday at lunchtime, because she has observed that a handful of church members meet there regularly to eat and visit.

When she walks in, the place gets quiet. When she walks over to say hello, her church members act awkward and standoffish. They aren't rude by any means, but they also don't ask her to join them. Sheepishly, she excuses herself, goes over to the counter, orders a sandwich to go, and then leaves. Driving back to her office, she feels foolish, embarrassed, and discouraged. *I don't know why I even try? They just don't like me. They're never going to even give me a chance. They think because I'm a woman that I don't know what I'm doing. Maybe I don't? Maybe I can't do this—maybe I should go back to teaching. A competent minister—a dynamic leader—wouldn't have these troubles.*

How would you describe her mind-set? Negative? "Woe is me?" Harshly self-critical? Defeated? Assuming the worst? Insecure? Self-pitying? Inferior?

True confession: I can relate. Much of my life I saw myself as inferior to others and unimportant: *Who do I think I am to suppose that I could _____ or _____.* That self-critical mind-set hindered me in my most important goals. It was a constant obstacle to fulfilling God's mission in my life. I have faced this negative mind-set at every significant milestone.

In writing this book, I once again had to confront the remnants of those stubborn feelings of inferiority. *What do you know?* the voices would hiss. *Why would people want to read about your experience or research?* I found myself dragging my feet continually. Though I really desired to help and encourage pastors, thoughts such as, *Do I really know what I am talking about?* or *Do I have anything important to say?* evidenced my self-doubt.

What did I do? I practiced the skill of resetting my mind-set. Here's a formula showing what that involves:

**Adjusting Self-Talk + Remembering Your Identity = Mind-Set Reset**

Let's break down each part.

### Adjusting Self-Talk

In a letter to the ancient Christians at Corinth (who had *lots* of struggles), the apostle Paul mentioned the idea of "taking every thought captive" (2 Cor. 10:5 NASB). It's a fascinating phrase. It pictures a team of guards patrolling our minds looking for stray thoughts that don't belong or that are up to no good. The idea is that whenever we come upon one of these renegade, unwelcome, unhelpful thoughts, we should apprehend it, take it away, lock it up, and throw away the key.

Emotionally intelligent leaders do a version of this. They monitor the commentary that takes place in their heads and ask questions of each thought, questions like:

- **Is it true?** Does it square with God's Word?
- **Is it accurate?** Do my thoughts here take into account all the facts? Do I have evidence to support my self-talk? Am I merely engaging in speculation, exaggerations, and wild assumptions?

- ◉ **Is it helpful?** Is my current way of thinking motivating or demotivating? Am I using unhelpful words like *can't*, *must*, or *should*?
- ◉ **Would others agree?** Would other wiser, more objective people agree with the statements I am telling myself here? Is there another way to view this situation?

As Pastor Bill began to examine his own habits of self-talk, he realized a few things. For example, he thought of a recent meeting in which he had received some mild criticism for allowing the youth pastor to preach the last Sunday in July. Bill had seen this as a way to help further the young man's training and help him develop credibility with the flock and his teaching gifts at a low-key time of year. Bill left that meeting shaking his head and thinking: *I can never please these people. No matter what I do, it's never right.* Consequently, he went into a 24-hour emotional funk, binge watching TV and leaving Celeste feeling even more irritated with him.

But now as he reflected, Bill realized that his self-talk about a couple of mildly critical comments had been exaggerations—gross exaggerations! He'd had at least four youth parents commend him for giving Kevin a chance to speak! What's more, the

**DANGEROUS PHRASES**

Saying "I can't" typically leads to feelings of powerlessness, anxiety, and even depression. I ask people to swap the phrase "I can't" for "I am having difficulty." Most find it difficult at first to overcome the "I can't" habit. They may even say, "I can't stop saying I can't!" However, when they get the hang of it, the result is a slight shifting in their emotional state. Suddenly, there's a sliver of hope and possibility, where moments before there had been only resignation and hopelessness. The effect of one simple change on our emotional responses is amazing.

Other phrases such as "I must" or "I should" are also dangerous. They create pressure to perform, be perfect, or overwork. The effect of an endless list of shoulds is exhaustion and feelings of hopelessness. Who can do everything, much less do everything right?

"I will never" is another catch phrase that sets us up for likely embarrassment, guilt, and shame.

entire youth group had crowded into the first three rows of the center section to show their love and support—completely changing the dynamic of the service for the better. And the greater truth? This kind of criticism was rare. People were almost always on board with Bill's ideas.

*Next time,* he thought, *I'm going to do a better job of taking thoughts captive.*

## Remembering Your Identity

Much of our self-talk is rooted in how we see ourselves. And much about the way we see ourselves comes from cues and clues—some good, but many bad—that we've picked up from the world around us—from parents, siblings, neighbors, teachers, spouses, friends, classmates, coaches, bosses, culture—as we've moved through life.

Robert McGee correctly observed that most people base their identity and self-worth on how well they measure up to others' opinions and expectations.[4] So, for example, if you hit the winning layup at the buzzer, you're a hero and a star. Miss it, however, and you're a bum and a loser. In such a brutal, unforgiving, performance-based system, your identity can change from day to day, and your feelings of self-worth can fluctuate like the stock market.

The message of the Bible is that we get our identity and worth from what God says is true about us. Period. In other words, we don't give ourselves an identity. Nor does the world around us determine our worth. God tells us who we are. *He* names us.

This is huge. It means our worth is not a matter of how we *feel* in a high or low moment, and it isn't tied to how well we *perform* our jobs or to the opinions of others. We are significant because of who we are in Christ.

Emotionally healthy pastors live from this mind-set. They trust what God says is true of them—that they are valuable, significant, and loved unconditionally. This worth isn't due to anything they have done or not done. Rather, it's because God gave them this identity when he created them in his image.

But more than giving us dignity, the gospel tells us that God gave us his Son. Jesus came, lived a perfect life, and died a terrible death—for us. Do you see? We are the exquisite creations of God (see Eph. 2:10). And by faith in his Son, we are God's children (see John 1:12)! In Christ, we enjoy the status of being unconditionally loved and fully accepted (see Romans 15:7).

The Lord speaks of our new, true identity all through Scripture. Among other things, he calls believers "saints" (Eph. 1:1 NASB), his "friends" (John 15:15), his "co-workers" (2 Cor. 6:1), and "members" of his body (1 Cor. 12:27 NASB). To illustrate how he is the ultimate bestower of identity—and how he is able to redirect a life—the Lord often changed the names of people in Scripture. Abram became Abraham. God changed Sarai's name to Sarah. He renamed Jacob, which means "deceiver," Israel. Simon became Peter, the "rock." The Lord renamed Saul, Paul.

Remember fearful Gideon, hiding from the enemy down in a wine-press? Imagine his shock when God's angel addressed him as "mighty warrior" (Judg. 6:12)! Clearly, God saw more in Gideon than he ever saw in himself.

It might be good to pause here and take a few minutes to reflect on the following identity questions:

- How do you typically view yourself?
- Who does God say that you are?
- Is the way you are currently seeing yourself helping or hindering your ministry?
- What, if any, changes do you need to make in your understanding of your identity?

Mastery of mind-set is not only learning to think rightly about people and situations, it's also learning to see ourselves as God sees us.

This skill helps us stay positive, encouraged, and moving toward our goals. It also helps us avoid assorted pitfalls, including resentment, the frantic need to prove ourselves, seeking our worth from how well we perform, being driven by fear of failure or rejection, trying to control people or outcomes, and letting others "name" us.

### Skill 2: Managing Emotional Triggers

A second habit that is critical to personal mastery is learning to manage emotional triggers. These hot buttons are situations in which we have an instinctive knee-jerk or exaggerated reaction. They are unique to each of us. A comment or happening that wouldn't even register on your conscious mind, might send shock waves through my soul—and vice versa. Much like a rip current in the ocean, we don't see these powerful triggers coming, and they are able to take us places we never were meant to go.

How can you better manage your emotional triggers? Here are four ways to develop this crucial habit.

#### Identify Your Unique Personal Triggers and Reactions

Before you can manage a thing, you first have to know what it is you are trying to manage. This was the goal of the "Know Your Hot Buttons Tool" in the chapter on personal insight.

#### Review Situations

Take a few minutes to assess a recent interaction or incident in which you definitely overreacted. Maybe you rushed from a room in embarrassment. Maybe in seconds your mood suddenly switched from upbeat to downcast. Describe the situation. What specifically triggered the sudden surge or change of emotion? As best as you can recall, what kind of self-talk and feelings were swirling in your head and heart at the time?

Life events often unfold suddenly—bringing a jumble of thoughts and feelings. And often in real-time—before you have the chance to process what just hit you—you are facing the next situation or interaction. The point being, it takes intentionality and time to cultivate the important habit of reviewing events so as to analyze your mind-set and related reactions.

## Take Time to Consider

As you get better at identifying your personal triggers and reaction patterns, you will develop the capacity to "call time out" for the purpose of cooling down and regaining objectivity and perspective. Instead of flying off the handle, you'll learn to say things like, "Let me take some time to think about all you've said and get back to you on it."

## Plan Ahead

Anticipate potential problems in advance so that you can head them off at the pass. Granted, many situations arise out of the blue, and there's no way to anticipate them or prepare. However, many situations are predictable and avoidable.

For example, before Pastor Jim meets Greg for coffee, he'll plan ahead. How so? By reflecting on what's true, reviewing recent history, and reminding himself of multiple truths:

- Greg is known and respected for being a levelheaded, reasonable, and spiritually mature guy. He wouldn't have such a reputation if he didn't have the character to match.
- Greg *did* have more influence during the tenure of the previous pastor, who was a less forceful leader than Jim. Perhaps he fears

losing influence. This does not excuse anything, but it might explain some things.

◉ Greg has been under severe stress at home and at work. Jim needs to remember this and show grace. The words sometimes attributed to Plato come to mind: "Be kind, for everyone you meet is fighting a hard battle."

◉ Greg's hesitation to Jim's plan just might be God's sovereign way of getting the board to put the brakes on a premature initiative (see Prov. 15:22). Jim needs to hold his agenda with an open hand.

◉ God is well able to shift Greg's heart. That means Jim doesn't need to push harder; he needs to pray more.

By prayerfully reviewing these facts before their coffee meeting, Jim feels calmer and less susceptible to being triggered. Instead of seeing Greg as an adversary and their different viewpoints as a battle to be won through arguing and powering up, he is able to see Greg as an ally, and their situation as a problem to be solved through listening, understanding, and building trust.

Here's the truth: The more you know your trigger tendencies, the more you review interactions for how you might have responded differently, and the more you preview potential trigger situations in advance, the more equipped you will be. Planning ahead is a combination of reviewing past events and rehearsing future interactions.

## Skill 3: Communicating Directly

A third skill of leaders who possess personal mastery is the practice of communicating directly.

It goes without saying that there are all sorts of communication styles and not all of them are healthy.

## Avoid Passive, Aggressive, and Passive–Aggressive Communication

You probably have people in your church who employ a *passive* communication style. "Boy, I sure do miss some of the old hymns we used to sing" is their round-about way of suggesting a change in the worship music. The problem is most people are oblivious to vague hints and subtlety, and others are more likely to feel irritated.

Perhaps this is your default communication style? How can you tell? What are the hallmarks of a passive communicator? You tend to bite your tongue more than you should. You don't have a lot of confidence, so you're reluctant to speak up or speak out. You tend to let others walk over you rather than stand up for yourself. You are likely to ignore offenses, even when they are egregious. The problem with this style is obvious. Passivity can lead to misunderstanding and frustration. Eventually it can culminate in a blowup.

Others are *passive-aggressive* in their communication. They won't look you in the eye and say what they really want to say. Instead, they communicate their displeasure in nonverbal, yet often loud, ways. Maybe they leave harsh, anonymous, handwritten notes on comment cards, making it impossible to have constructive, follow-up conversations. Or, in the case of the worship example given above, they wear neon-colored earplugs to church! (Don't laugh—such things happen!) Or they make it a point to wait not-so-subtly in the foyer each Sunday morning, dramatically refusing to enter the sanctuary until immediately after the worship music ends.

Take Tom as an example. He is unhappy with changes at his church. A long-time, faithful member, he's also hurt that that no one consulted him before those big decisions were made. Disgruntled and agitated, Tom decides to stop giving to the church as an expression of his dissatisfaction.

It's not hard to see the ineffectiveness of this type of "communication." First, it might be months before anyone even notices that Tom has stopped giving. When and if someone does notice, it's likely to be misinterpreted as "I'd better pray for Tom. He's apparently having some financial struggles!" How much better and more mature it would be for Tom to communicate his concerns directly to the elder board or a staff member! At least then his views would be heard in a timely and unambiguous way, and a discussion could be held. Perhaps both parties would benefit from new insights. Clearly, passive-aggressive communication leaves a lot to be desired.

Most of us, however, are guilty, at least on occasion. When asked, "What's wrong?" we say, "Nothing" with our mouths, even as our body language communicates, "Everything!" This kind of passive-aggressiveness may explain why your competent staff member can't seem to carry out a simple assignment. Or it may be the reason a board member signs off on a plan in a meeting, then leaves and does nothing to elicit support for the plan or help accomplish it.

To be fair, people embrace a passive-aggressive communication style sometimes, because they don't feel permission to verbalize their true opinions. It is worth asking the question, "Have we created a culture at our church where people feel muzzled, where they feel they'll be punished if they speak freely and honestly?"

Probably you have a few in your church (maybe even on your board) who employ an *aggressive* style of communication. You know the type. They say what they think. They're more blunt than tactful. Forget surgical strikes, they will carpet bomb you with words. They don't beat around the bush. Oftentimes these are competent, confident, type A, get-it-done type personalities. They aren't trying to be cruel. They are simply driven. They often accomplish great tasks—and leave a trail of bodies in their wake! This style—assuming one is better than the others—explains the way Pastor Jim has learned to function. Now he needs to learn a different way.

Jim, as we've seen, tends to be quite clear and direct in his communication. He carefully articulates his vision and strategies to his leadership. This really helps the team and congregation get on board and know what to do. At times, however, Jim can slip into a more aggressive communication style. This often occurs when he feels criticized, or when others disagree with him or seem to be holding up progress. In such cases, Jim's tendency is to shoot down any ideas that interfere with his plans and verbally override others. The result is that most staff and board members withhold valuable feedback and quietly become angry.

Examining his communication style, Jim decides that he needs to stop and listen more. He needs to reflect—not simply react—when others voice a differing opinion. Though this feels unnatural to him, he realizes how important this quality is for effective leadership. To help with this, he has decided to ask a member of his board whom he trusts to signal him when he starts overriding a conversation.

Pastor Bill, on the other hand, tends to naturally default to a passive communication style. Not wanting to upset others, he is disinclined to speak up or offer conflicting opinions or be assertive. It's really difficult for him to confront problem situations and set boundaries.

Upon examining his most recent conflict situation, he identified two alternate and more direct communication strategies he could have employed. First, he could have told the committee member that he was very sorry that he had overlooked this important Boys and Girls Club meeting. He could have stated that he had already obligated himself to another commitment and would not be available. Realizing the importance of the event, however, he would find a replacement to stand in for the meeting and be sure to record it in the calendar for next year. Though the committee member would have been unhappy, it would have worked out okay.

Alternately, if he had decided to go ahead and speak at the meeting, he could have spoken immediately to his wife about it. Though she would naturally have been upset, by telling her sooner perhaps another plan could have been created. Part of her anger was his knowing about the conflict and not telling her!

Passive communication, aggressive communication, passive-aggressive communication—all of these styles cause problems. Which is why EI leaders opt for direct communication.

## What Is Direct Communication?

Direct communication is calmly and respectfully but directly expressing what one thinks, feels, needs, or otherwise desires to have happen. This kind of communication is up front and clear—not vague or veiled, as with passive communication.

Unlike aggressive communication, which often starts with "You never" or "You always," direct communication doesn't put people on the defensive. It is characterized by "I" statements: "I think;" "I feel;" "I would like;" "I need."

In most situations, with a few exceptions, direct communication is the optimal communication style. Spelling out clearly what you think and feel is healthy for you and for your relationships. This doesn't mean *always* saying *everything* you think. Solomon wisely noted, "Sensible people control their temper; they earn respect by overlooking wrongs" (Prov. 19:11 NLT). Not every situation is worth debating. Not every flaw needs to be pointed out. Even when experiencing unfair criticism or mistreatment, we are called to turn the other cheek and to respond with love and blessing.

Praying for wisdom can assist us in knowing when it's best to overlook a problem and when it's right to address it. And this is important—overlooking an offense means letting it go, not "saving it for a rainy day" and stockpiling annoyance or resentment in the meantime. This only results in internal and external tension.

Being an EI leader means setting an example of direct communication. Obviously, you can't *make* other people stop being overly aggressive or passive-aggressive in their communication. But *you* can stop communicating in those unhealthy ways and model direct communication instead. This will mean:

- ⦿ Praying about *what* to say, *when*, and *how*. Timing and tone are huge. Sometimes we say the right things, but we say them in the wrong way or with the wrong spirit—or we say them before the other person is ready to hear them.
- ⦿ Rooting out all passive-aggressive behavior from your life. If you are frustrated with someone because of how they treated you in a meeting, talk to them about that incident; don't punish them by not responding to their email.
- ⦿ Mastering the powerful urge to shrink back and say nothing when you really need to speak up.
- ⦿ Overcoming the fear of how others might respond. Their response is not your concern; you are only responsible for your choices.
- ⦿ Resisting the strong but sinful desire to "let someone have it" for either doing or not doing something.
- ⦿ Being truthful and clear rather than evasive and ambiguous. In other words, EI leaders don't employ the old salesman/politician communication trick of the "snow job," blanketing others with a blizzard of words designed not to clarify, but to mislead, confuse, or avoid taking a definitive stand.

Don't let lazy, fear-based, dysfunctional, or immature communication habits corrupt your leadership. Experience the freedom of personal mastery by engaging in direct, honest, and sensitive communication. You will feel better about yourself. You'll also be setting the tone for healthy communication in the congregation.

Here is a simple example of what direct communication looks like. In this case, it involves Pastor Susan talking to the church pianist about her being chronically late for Wednesday night choir practice:

"Hey, Gwen, do you have a minute?"

"Sure, what's up?"

"Well, it's about choir practice."

"Um, what about it?"

"Well, I've had several members make comments about the practices starting late and running late recently."

Long pause.

"Yeah, I guess I've been fifteen to twenty minutes late the last few weeks."

"That's what I've heard. Let me ask this: Is there a conflict? I mean, do we need to move the practice time back thirty minutes or something? Would that help you?"

"No, I just need to be more organized. Leave the house sooner."

"I can relate. My schedule gets crazy too. Gwen, look, I know we're not paying you that much to lead worship, and I know that in the big eternal scheme of things, people having to wait twenty minutes may not seem like a huge deal. But here's the thing: When you're not there on time, the choir members feel frustrated. You know that feeling when the doctor keeps you waiting?"

"Yeah. That's irritating. I need to be more considerate. I'm sorry."

"I appreciate you saying that. Maybe you can tell the choir that next week? Not that anyone is mad, but it would probably be a good thing to do."

"I can do that."

"And so, you'll make it a priority to get there a few minutes early from now on?"

"I sure will."

"Awesome. Thanks, Gwen. I appreciate that, and I know the choir will too. And by the way, I don't know if I said this, but the special music you guys did Sunday was beautiful."

If you analyze Susan's words, you'll see a broad template for direct communication. It looks something like this:

- ◉ When you _____, I/we/others feel _____.
- ◉ I/we/others typically react by _____.
- ◉ What I/we would like is _____ (describe a better way for future interactions).

◉ This would help us both/all because _____ (describe
  benefits or potential consequences).
◉ Can we try this? (elicit cooperation).

## Reflection Questions

Here are some questions to help you reflect on your typical style of
communication.

◉ What would you say your default communication style is? (If
  you're not sure, ask your spouse or a trusted friend to give you
  feedback. Trust me—they'll know!)
◉ How do others typically react to your communication style?
  Positively? Negatively?
◉ In what current situation would it benefit you to utilize a more
  direct communication approach?
◉ If you could go back to your last tough conversation, what would
  you say differently? How would you better word your interaction?
◉ Are there some instances in which saying nothing is the best
  approach?

## *Skill 4: Maintaining Your Passion*

A fourth hallmark of those who have learned personal mastery is that
they maintain their passion. The apostle Paul expressed it this way in
his famous letter to first-century Christians in Rome: "Never be lacking
in zeal, but keep your spiritual fervor, serving the Lord" (Rom. 12:11).

Zeal, spiritual fervor, or passion is the spark that keeps us going. It's
why we started doing ministry in the first place. We experienced the
overwhelming love of God and felt a love for him. That spilled over into
a love for people. The internal urge to make an eternal difference, that

sense of spiritual enthusiasm—there's nothing like being full of holy passion. And yet, the grind of everyday busyness and church problems can wear us down over time and steal our zeal.

How does one do this—maintain spiritual fervor, remain zealous? Here are a few things that help us keep our heart fires burning:

- Letting the Lord minister to us when we are spiritually exhausted (see 1 Kings 19).
- Seeing God's Word as our ultimate source of vitality and refreshment (see Ps. 119).
- Asking God to fill us with his Spirit and to manifest in and through us the fruit of the Spirit (see Eph. 5:18 and Gal. 5:22–23).
- Taking Christ's yoke, not someone else's expectations, upon us (see Matt. 11:28–30).
- Making sure we take time to rest (see Mark 6:31).
- Being part of healthy community (see Acts 2:42–47). *In the same way that a glowing coal quickly dies out when it is alone on the hearth, so a solitary believer quickly loses his or her spark.*
- Being around and hearing about inspiring, Spirit-filled people (see examples in Acts 11:22–24 and 2 Cor. 9:2).
- Hearing stories about what God has done or is doing (see Acts 21:19–20).
- Praying honestly for passion—to be "filled to the measure of all the fullness of God" (Eph. 3:19).
- Remembering our union with Christ (see Phil. 2:1).

Practically, these biblical imperatives may include such daily, weekly, monthly, and annual activities as engaging in personal retreats, reading great books, and reading and meditating on Scripture. In addition, having hobbies that replenish us, having a group of friends with whom we can "be real," learning about new ministries, following inspiring people on social media or via podcasts, practicing Sabbath, setting up healthy boundaries, and saying no to certain things will aid in maintaining our passions.

## Reflection Questions

Here are some questions to help you reflect on maintaining your passion.

1. What are you most passionate about?
2. What areas of ministry excite and reinvigorate you?
3. What things drain you or de-energize you? Be specific. What is draining you this year, this month?
4. What things have re-energized you in the past or been helpful to renew yourself during or after a stressful event? Circle any or all that apply.

| | | |
|---|---|---|
| Time with friends | Sabbath | Journaling |
| Solitude | Spiritual direction | Travel |
| Time away (vacation) | Worship | Prayer |
| Retreats | Involvement in mission | Service |
| Naps | Exercise · | Manual labor |
| Counseling | Sabbaticals | Other: |
| Reading | Hobbies | |

5. Just for fun: If you came to see *you* for pastoral counseling, what would you say?
6. Based on your answers above, brainstorm some options for doing more of the things you love, and less of the things you don't do well or that drain your energy and passion.
7. If you are in a season of stress or burnout, based on your answers to question number four, what could you change?

Take a step: Identify one thing you are going to attempt in order to increase your passion. When will you take this step? What is your deadline?

## Toward Greater Personal Mastery

The apostle Paul issued this warning: "So, if you think you are standing firm, be careful that you don't fall!" (1 Cor. 10:12). That sentence ought to send a shiver down every leader's spine. Frankly, we've all got "stuff" that could make us fall. We each have issues we need to work on. Pastor Bill needs to learn how to avoid giving in to dark thoughts. Pastor Susan needs to better monitor the self-talk in her head. Pastor Jim needs to learn to avoid giving in to anger and frustration. If he goes forward with humility and wisdom, he can surely survive the recent blowup he had with Greg and his board. But he probably can't survive many more outbursts. None of these pastors can afford to let their weaknesses go unaddressed. Neither can you and I.

We don't have to suppress our emotions or surrender to them. We can regulate and even alter our emotions. We can calm ourselves when angry, encourage ourselves when discouraged, and act with confidence even when we feel anxious. We can master our emotions—and we must master them, or they will master us. It's that simple.

The struggle is worth it. It pays big dividends. Self-mastery elevates you to a higher level of performance and leadership. It means your "stuff" won't come back to bite you in the you-know-what! When you engage in difficult situations you will keep your wits about you. Your emotions won't be driving you. You won't be at the mercy of other people's drama. You will stay passionate, disciplined, and effectual. You will operate at your highest potential.

My challenge to you is to identify the personal tendencies that are hindering your growth as a leader. Assess yourself. Come up with a plan to address your deficiencies. List some measurable, specific goals and "calendarize" them. That is, set some dates out there as targets. Then, get busy working on personal mastery! It's only by learning personal mastery that we are able to live with freedom and power.

# Acquiring Relational Insight

At the pastors' conference, Susan felt like she was drinking from the proverbial fire hose. By the end, her hand was actually sore from scribbling notes nonstop for three days! So many great ideas, thoughts, insights, and resources!

RELATIONAL
INSIGHT

Thanks to the content shared in the plenary sessions and in her "Women in Ministry" track, Susan felt challenged, but also hopeful. All the big-name speakers seemed to have their own horror stories—and they were still standing and serving!

Being in a group with Jim and Bill had been a blessing too. Their stories were eye opening and prompted thoughts like, *The ministry is tough for every pastor—no matter how experienced or gifted! The problems and pressures don't stop—they just take on different forms.*

Susan felt oddly encouraged after hearing about their unique challenges: *At least I'm not the only one struggling. Everybody has things— internal and external—to work on. And the grass isn't greener. People are people no matter where you go. Having a bigger church, a larger staff and budget, or more talented musicians wouldn't solve my problems—it would just present me with a different set of challenges.*

One of Susan's biggest takeaways was this realization (written in the front of her conference notebook):

**I'm a city girl in a country church!** So, *if* I feel totally out of my element—it's because I *am* out of my element! But that's okay. Being out of my comfort zone forces me to lean on the Lord and to remember Paul's words, "When I am weak, then I am strong" (2 Cor. 12:10). And in 2 Corinthians 3 (NASB), "Not that I'm adequate in myself . . . my adequacy comes from God."

Young, fresh out of seminary, progressive in mind-set, the first female pastor in the church's history, unaccustomed to rural life and the ways of a small farming community—is it surprising that Susan got off to a slow start in her ministry? Or that she and her congregation didn't instantly bond?

Post-conference, Susan embraced a new approach. Rather than trying to implement a bunch of new programs or preach rousing sermons (she had been in her study those first months, prepping more than twenty hours a week!), she began focusing almost all her efforts on simply getting to know her people and the town of Claymore, Kansas. She started taking the initiative, dropping by homes and offices just to say hello, engaging people, asking for gardening advice (which most neighbors were glad to give), making coffee appointments, eating lunch in the diner, making and delivering her one-of-a-kind, to-die-for brownies to the nursing home, church members, and city officials.

Since she's not a true extrovert, being this outgoing hasn't been easy for Susan. Some days she has to force herself out the door to go meet someone new. But every time she does, she's glad after the fact that she did so. And every time she walks away thinking, *I never would have known that. . . .*

This intentional "listening tour" is growing Susan's heart for her community. It is spurring her prayer life. It's helping her feel connected. It's causing people to open up to her. It's giving her the credibility and a platform to speak words of hope and life. Imagine Susan's shock one night recently on the way home from a high school basketball game when she turned to her husband and said, "After two months I was ready to pack up and leave this place. Now, honestly, I'm in love with Claymore!"

## What Is Relational Insight?

Relational insight is the ability to be in tune with others, to hear their hearts, read their moods, feel their pain, and understand their perspective. At a group level, it is an awareness of the dynamics and mood "in the room." It is understanding at a deep level the culture of the congregation. While some leaders seem to have a special, God-given ability for connecting in these ways, these are interpersonal skills that anyone can develop.

## Relational Insight Challenges

The influential author, speaker, and church planter Ed Stetzer has asserted that pastors "need to know our culture and context and engage it well."[1]

Never was a truer word spoken! Whether being relatively new in a congregation (like pastors Susan and Jim) or being in a long-term congregational relationship (like Pastor Bill) a spiritual leader has multiple relational challenges to consider. To be effective he or she needs:

◉ Some personal knowledge of what is going on with individual members of the congregation and in the lives of the leadership or staff team

◉ Insight into the congregation as a whole: its unique history, culture, personality, values, and how the members function corporately

◉ An understanding of the inner workings and dynamics of the leadership team and what happens when those diverse, gifted individuals get in a room together

◉ A good sense or feel for the larger community, the context in which the congregation lives and ministers. Is it urban, suburban, or rural? What are the demographics, history, strengths, and unique challenges, whether racial, socio-economic, educational, or something else?

In a sense, relational insight involves being a careful observer of people—individuals and groups—keeping one's ear to the ground and staying connected. It is becoming a student of the culture in which one finds oneself.

## Why Does Relational Insight Matter?

Relational insight is important for at least five reasons.

### God Models Relational Insight with Us

The Old Testament claims that God knows us through and through, that he constantly sees us and keeps up with us. In Psalm 139:18 we read that his thoughts of us outnumber the grains of sand on the seashore! In Isaiah 49:16, we come across the breathtaking image of God engraving the names of his people on the palm of his hand!

In the New Testament Jesus is our model for leadership empathy. No one ever understood human nature better, and no one ever showed more compassion. He not only was tempted "in every way, just as we are" (Heb. 4:15), he was continually touched and moved as he observed the real needs of real people (see Matt. 20:34; Mark 6:34; John 11:38).

As God's children and Christ's followers we are fully known, loved, and understood. What a comfort! It's no wonder that as spiritual leaders called to emulate Christ, we are to move toward others to know them. What a challenge! Like Jesus our Good Shepherd, we must seek to understand and address the needs of those in our flocks.

## Relational Insight Gives Us a Voice with Others

Speaking effectively into someone's wounded heart, or deftly addressing the needs of a diverse congregation or its wider culture, necessitates being in touch with people. Without a finger on others' emotional and spiritual pulse, our messages will be irrelevant at best, tone-deaf at worst. Good leaders understand the concerns and fears and empathize with the hopes and aspirations of those they seek to lead.

This is hard work. It takes time. But when we develop our relational capacity with the help and guidance of the Holy Spirit, we are more effective. Our words resonate. People are touched at a deep level.

Relationship insight is invaluable in leading staff teams and working with board members. Knowing your fellow leaders and the unique ways they interact provides insight for the formulation of vision and strategy. This knowledge can help defuse conflicts and build effective teams.

## Relational Insight Is Essential to Good Relationships

The movie *Remember the Titans* tells the true story of how a high school football coach, played by Denzel Washington, brought his racially divided football team together by making them bunk together during a grueling, preseason training camp. As these young men practiced and sweated together by day and goofed off together by night, they gained a better understanding of one other. Their suspicions and prejudices faded. Bonds of friendship and trust formed. As a result—spoiler alert—the team won the championship! Hollywood embellishments aside, the basic premise of the film is true. When we take the time to get to know others, more often than not, we develop a greater appreciation for them. And we are usually able to do greater things together as a result.

## Relational Insight Is Essential to Effective Leadership

Most of us have been in a situation—whether in our family, school, workplace, or elsewhere—when we felt misunderstood or ignored by those "in control." Is anything more frustrating and demotivating than when leadership or management turns a deaf ear or when they act in tone-deaf ways? And yet, think of other situations—when you felt an authority figure really cared about you, took the time to listen and under-stand, and demonstrated genuine interest. Is anything more empowering and inspiring? You would follow that kind of leader anywhere!

## Relational Insight Is the Only Sane Basis for Team Vision and Strategy

Imagine a football coach deciding to install a particular type of offense without even bothering to look first at his roster. Wouldn't it help him to know up front that he doesn't have a quarterback who can throw the ball worth a flip or that his receivers are slow and not really gifted at catching the ball? Knowing your people's strengths, weaknesses, and personalities is indispensable to formulating wise vision and strategies that will actually work. This is as true in ministry as it is in sports.

## The Skills of Relational Insight

As with the other components of emotional intelligence that we have looked at, personal insight and personal mastery, those with high *relational insight* have cultivated certain skills.

## Skill 1: Listening

It's been said that the top priority of any new pastor in their first year at a church should be getting to know the people in the congregation, the history, traditions, and culture of the church and surrounding community—and letting them get to know the pastor. Through her rocky start, followed by a very intentional "listening tour," Susan learned just how true this is.

Is it a biblical command for pastors to drink coffee with parishioners or to take brownies to the fire station? Uh, . . . not really. However, the Scripture does exhort us to be "quick to listen" and "slow to speak" (James 1:19). Investing time in getting to know the people we seek to minister to just makes sense. In his best-selling classic *The Seven Habits of Highly Effective People*, Stephen Covey conveyed a similar message: "Seek first to understand, then to be understood."[2]

Let's be honest. When it comes to listening, our culture deserves a collective F. And sometimes as pastors, we're not much better. Most people, most of the time, are more focused on expressing their views than hearing the views of others. If we feel like we are not being heard, we get louder and louder and more and more frustrated. Soon, we're just shouting past each other! Even when we're not speaking, we have a natural tendency to mentally rehearse what we're going to say next as soon as the other person pauses to take a breath. We are not natural listeners, but we can learn this important skill.

## Basic Listening Skills

Here are some simple practices that can help you develop this all-important relational trait.

- **Focus on the person**—Turn your chair, angle your body, physically face the person. This kind of body language communicates priority and concern.
- **Make eye contact**—Avoid looking out the window, or at the cellphone on your desk, or at the TV on the wall across the room. Eye contact communicates engagement.
- **Fix your mind on what is being said**—Resist the urge to "mentally multitask." Turn off your inner self-talk, push the pause button on your previous train of thought. When your mind starts to wander, lasso it, and bring it back to the conversation at hand. Tune out everything but what the other person is saying.
- **Ask a pertinent, open-ended question**—Ask, "Can you say that again? Would you tell me a little more about that?" This communicates interest, and it affords you the chance to glean more information.
- **Reflect back what you heard**—Say, "I want to make sure I'm understanding you. You're saying _____. Is that accurate? Did I hear you correctly?" If the other person responds affirmatively and becomes more engaged in response to your questions, you're doing a good job of listening. Keep it up! If they shake their head in disgust, throw a couch pillow at you, or walk away in frustration, you probably need to try again!

These practices and exercises may not seem like much. They are pretty basic. However, they can help you hear more than you would have, even if you already are a pretty good listener.

## A Listening Experiment

Here is a reminder and a challenge. Reading about listening won't make you a better listener, just like watching a golf tournament on TV won't improve your handicap. You have to take action. You have to practice the right skills. If you really want to build new and better listening habits, do the following experiment.

- Before your head hits the pillow tonight, think of a situation, event, project, prayer request, or something else that someone in your life—a spouse, colleague, child, parishioner, or neighbor—has mentioned to you.
- As soon as you can, initiate a conversation about that matter or item by saying, "Hey, the other day, you mentioned _____. Give me an update on that. What's the latest?" Then use all the listening skills outlined above.
- Focus on reflective listening: "It sounds like you are saying _____." In other words, summarize what they have said, being careful not to inject your own ideas or feelings. Ask, "Did I understand you correctly?"
- After this conversation, take out a pen and paper as soon as possible and write down everything you can remember about the conversation. Ask and answer the question, "What could I have done differently? Better?"

## Listening Truths for Leaders

Leaders can benefit from understanding two listening truths:

First, no leader can possibly know everything that is going on in his or her organization. Yet every leader can ask his or her people good questions and listen carefully and intently to the answers. This practice always leads to greater insight.

Second, when people feel listened to, they feel loved and cared for.

Recently a network newscast reported on a group of high school kids who are using their culinary interests and skills to prepare food for the homeless in a major US city. One homeless man said that while the food was delicious, what he loved most about this program was how the kids would come out after the meal and sit with him and the others and listen to their stories. When people feel heard, they feel loved. Listening communicates "You matter" and "I care." When we don't listen well, the conclusion others draw is "You don't care" or "You care about other things more." Ouch!

### Skill 2: Tuning In to Others

A second characteristic of leaders who possess high levels of relational insight is that they have learned the skill of tuning in to others. The question arises, How is this different from listening?

More than listening, *tuning in* entails paying careful attention to changes or shifts in others or in a congregation. You put your radar up. You observe people. You "read" them. You put yourself in the place of others. You try to get on the same frequency with them emotionally. This allows you to empathize, to see things from their perspective, and ultimately to grow in your understanding of what it feels like to be that person. Tuning in to others is what Paul had in mind when he urged the Roman believers, "Be happy with those who are happy, and weep with those who weep" (Rom. 12:15 NLT).

Specifically, when you "tune in," you pay close attention to

◉ **Unspoken words**. What is she saying through sighs, moans, or pauses. In addition to the obvious, note the subtext and context, the mood, the atmosphere, the vibe.

- **Body language.** Is his head down? Is her posture open or closed? Are they standing straight and tall or stooped? Be mindful, though, that body language will differ—and mean different things—from culture to culture.
- **Facial expressions.** Are his eyes closed? Moist? Flashing? Is his jaw clenched? Is she smiling? If so, is the smile genuine and unforced? Genuine smiles include the eyes, whereas a forced smile doesn't. On this topic, I highly recommend Paul Ekman's brilliant book *Emotions Revealed.*
- **Voice tone.** Are there changes in inflection? Pitch? Volume?
- **Other cues.** Are there subtle or abrupt changes in actions, demeanor, or personal hygiene?
- **The "feel" of a room.** Is the atmosphere electric? Tense? Somber? Nervous?

This reading of people—tuning in to their concerns, struggles, and feelings—is indispensable to good relationships because of the old maxim that people don't care how much you know until they know how much you care. Tuning in is really about being a student of people. The better you know someone and the closer you pay attention, the more you will notice subtle changes on the surface of their lives. And these things can be important clues to bigger things going on in their hearts.

Here are some key ways to sharpen your ability to tune in to people and groups.

## Play "Conversational Detective"

Enter each conversation with your curiosity meter turned up to "10." Observe. Take mental notes. Pay attention to *everything* mentioned above. Afterwards, write down not only the content of the conversation, but exactly what you saw and felt.

## Put Yourself in the Other's Shoes

Ask yourself the empathy question, If this were happening to me, how would I feel?

It's a great question to ponder before, during, and after you sit with a congregant or some other person—in a counseling session, coffee shop, funeral home, hospital room, courtroom, or anywhere else. The point isn't to project your feelings onto the other person, but to enter into their experience with them.

## Practice Reflective Listening

Repeat, in the form of a question, the sentiments you heard the other person expressing. Here's an example: When Susan was discussing her difficulties "breaking through" to her new congregation, Jim said, "So it sounds like they view you as an outsider who wants to change the way 'we've always done things around here.'" That's reflective listening.

## Get Your "Yes"

In reflective listening, you restate the other person's position until he or she agrees that you have accurately summarized it to his or her satisfaction. You wait for the other person to acknowledge that your perception of what he or she is saying and feeling is accurate. To Jim's reflections above, Susan might say, "Yes, that's exactly how they view me!"

Getting to "yes" is important, because once others are able to say, "Finally, yes! Someone understands!" they are more likely to continue talking. Even if they first say, "No, that's not quite it," you can ask follow-up questions and seek further clarity. This will communicate that you really do care and really do desire to understand and sympathize.

I know very few sure-fire formulas in this life, but here's one I've seen among pastors with high emotional intelligence:

Listening + Tuning In to Others = Acquiring Relational Insight

## Skill 3: Knowing Your Team

The most effective leaders spend time getting to know their teams.

Who is on your "team"? Is it your board, your paid staff, a task force, or a group of volunteer lay leaders? All of the above? Here's what I know: A leader really needs his or her team. Teams are not only a great source of support; more importantly, they are the ones who are going to help you effectively implement your mutual vision and ministry objectives. Behind every great leader is an exceptional team.

This is why emotionally intelligent leaders make it a priority to get to know their teams intimately. This is mandatory—not optional—for every pastor. As we saw with Pastor Susan, this is especially critical for new pastors.

What are the best ways for a leader to get to know his or her team? You might start by thinking about all the individuals in your group and then asking and answering these questions:

1. What are the personalities?
2. Do certain personalities clash?
3. Who tends to play the devil's advocate?
4. Who tends play the role of peacemaker?
5. Who loves to generate ideas?
6. Who always asks questions?
7. Who has to be encouraged to speak up, but has a lot to share when they do?
8. Who has the most power and why? Who is most influential?

Next, thinking of the group as a whole, spend some time reflecting on these questions:

1. What is the vibe when the group gets together?
2. How well do they know each other?
3. What history—good and bad—do the team members share?
4. Do they seem to enjoy—or merely tolerate—each other?
5. Is this team able to debate ideas vigorously without falling into personal attacks and petty arguments?

Getting to know your team will take effort and time. Having one meeting every other week can be a challenge! Time for just "hanging out" is even harder to come by. What can you do?

Plan an activity that will help you and your team get to know each other better. Possibilities include:

- Having your entire team take the Myers-Briggs inventory or the DISC personality assessment and debrief.
- Picking out a pertinent book to read and discuss together.
- Eating together. Maybe have a potluck or cook-out dinner once a month for the next six months. Don't stress or get discouraged if people have conflicts and have to miss. Whoever shows, shows.
- Spending a Friday night camping or a Saturday canoeing or doing a ropes course together.
- Taking a road trip together to a leadership conference in a nearby city.
- Going on a mission trip together.

It doesn't matter where you start; try something—anything—to foster closer relationships.

## Skill 4: Learning the Landscape

The fourth habit of leaders with high relational insight is that they take the time and make the effort to understand the unique history and culture of their congregation and community. In the same way that people have fascinating backstories, so do churches and cities.

This only makes sense. You would never head out on a hike without taking the time first to study the terrain. And you'd probably be hopelessly lost if you skipped seasons one through three of a TV series and jumped straight into season four.

Make the effort to become more knowledgeable about your congregation's unique context and backstory. Every pastor should acquire this knowledge—and new pastors should make this priority one. I've known clergy who, more than twenty years into a pastorate, were still learning new things about their people and community!

How does one go about this task? I suggest finding a few honest, trustworthy old-timers; asking lots of questions; and listening intently. The following questions are simple conversation starters. You can surely think of others. The point is to investigate and pay close attention. What you learn can save you many headaches and much heartache. Knowing about the past can help you make sense of the present and give you guidance for the future.

- What do you know about the history of this church?
- What have been its high points? Its hardest moments?
- What were the strengths and weaknesses of your former pastors?
- What were the smartest or best decisions ever made by your previous pastors?
- What do you think is the most important part of a pastor's job?
- What would the previous pastor say was the best part of pastoring this church? And what was hardest part?

◉ What percentage of the congregation would you say is happy with the direction the church is going? What percentage is unhappy? What are they most happy (or unhappy) about?

◉ Whom do you consider the most influential leaders in this congregation?

◉ What five words would you use to describe this body?

◉ If the congregation were asked that same question, how would they describe themselves?

Can you think of three church members you'd feel comfortable inviting to drink coffee and asking these questions? When will you set up your first appointment?

## Toward Greater Relational Insight

Relational insight enables you to connect deeply with others and have influence with them. If you don't know or understand your people, you cannot possibly hope to speak into their lives.

What will happen if you choose the easy way and don't make a concerted effort to work on your relational insight skills? Nothing! Sadly, that's exactly what will happen. Oh, they may listen politely to your homilies. They may smile and nod when you speak with them.

However, if you do not really understand what is going on in your personal relationships or in the group dynamics of your organization, ultimately you will be seen as irrelevant. You will have very little influence.

As I've said before, the very fact that you have picked up this book indicates your desire for deeper impact. Bless you! May your tribe increase!

Right now, ask God for a deeper commitment to know your people better than ever. Determine to increase your understanding of how they see the world and where they are spiritually, what things wake them up at night, and what hopes keep them going. Resolve to study your congregation and learn its unique history and dynamics.

My challenge to you: Identify two specific things you will do to improve or increase your relational insight. Then decide when you will do them!

# 8

# Cultivating Relational Mastery

As Jim eased into his garage following the pastors' conference, he was surprised at how much his heart had shifted. When he had backed out of his garage only a few days earlier to go to the conference, he'd been more than a little angry. He'd been ticked at Greg and frustrated by the board's unwillingness to stand up to him. He had also been embarrassed at the way he'd acted in the board meeting.

RELATIONAL MASTERY

Now, arriving back home, he felt remorseful that he'd so quickly judged everyone and been so critical. He realized there were several things he needed to do.

First, he needed to have some meetings—with Greg in the morning and with the board on Thursday night. His only agenda? To express how sorry he was for his blowup and to ask for a reset on their personal and working relationships.

He prayerfully concluded he would,

- humble himself by refusing to engage in any finger-pointing, blame-shifting, rationalizing, justifying, or making excuses for his actions;

◉ focus only on his wrong attitudes and actions;

◉ solicit honest feedback about his leadership—and listen to it, no matter how uncomfortable it made him;

◉ seek to understand other viewpoints without arguing or defending his own; and

◉ reiterate his desire to be allies.

More than wanting to "get his own way," Jim wanted his board to be a unified team "loving one another, and working together with one mind and purpose" (Phil. 2:2 NLT).

He hoped that such an authentic *mea culpa* would serve as a springboard for a constructive discussion. Jim wrote down his thoughts so that he could clarify them:

I need to go back and re-ask some of the questions we talked about when I was first interviewing for this position. I need to inquire again about their hopes for the church and their expectations of me as pastor. And I need to LISTEN intently! I really need to hear them out. Hopefully, that will de-escalate any tensions, and it will help me understand more clearly and allow them to feel listened to. If tensions still seem high or it doesn't go well, we can always call in a mediator to help us navigate the situation—though I doubt that'll be necessary.

I thought the church wanted certain changes and that we had created a shared vision and were ready to move on that. Clearly there's been a disconnect between my expectations and those of others. I need to spell out what I thought I had been hearing them express regarding our corporate vision and goals—and let them clarify.

We don't have to be in a rush to nail this down. I don't want to get impatient. More than we need to be moving down the road, we need consensus that we're on the right road and moving toward an agreed-upon destination.

........................................................

Jim's got a bold and gutsy plan, and it will require lots of humility. But he is exercising emotionally intelligent leadership. He has a good heart, and he's a strong and persuasive communicator.

I predict that by Friday morning, Jim will be in a much better place with Greg and the rest of the board. What's more, he'll be in a better place internally. And the church will be better positioned to make a difference in Denver—and throughout the world.

## What Is Relational Mastery?

Relational mastery is the ability to manage relationships wisely. When we infuse this skill with God's anointing, it leads to true transformational ministry.

For leaders, especially pastoral leaders who love people and want to influence them for eternal good, this is the fun part of emotional intelligence. This is where all our hard work pays off.

All those insights into what makes us tick and what ticks us off; all that getting a grip on our emotional triggers; all that listening to people and tuning in to groups to figure out what's really going on in their hearts under the surface—all that is just worthless information unless and until we put it into practice.

That is where relational mastery comes in. Relational mastery is where we take all our newly acquired self-awareness and "people smarts" and engage skillfully with others. With God-supplied insight and wisdom, we manage our relationships and interactions. With discernment, we lead individuals and teams through difficulties and change. It is this kind of wise pastoral care that builds trust. So that when we communicate vision, we discover people "buying in" and experiencing life change.

We could say it this way:

......................................................

**Emotional Intelligence + Connection with God = Transformational Ministry!**

......................................................

## *Why Does Relational Mastery Matter?*

The answer to this question may be obvious, but let me quickly mention five reasons this skill is so important.

### God Cares Deeply About Our Relationships

God, in his very nature—his *triune* nature—is relational, and we are made in his image (see Gen. 1:26–28). We were designed for relationship. When asked to name the most important of the 613 Old Testament laws, Jesus boiled them all down to one simple relational rule: love God and love people (see Mark 12:29–31). As leaders, this is our calling: to move toward people and help them move toward God. No wonder God cares so much about the people in our ministries. He made them! He loves them! He knows and understands them, even when we don't! He calls us to feed and lead his people—and promises to give us whatever we need in order to do so. He expects our best.

## Leadership Effectiveness Is Directly Tied to Relationships

Leading any group of people toward any goal is easier said than done. Leading a group of church people might even be more difficult. This is because people in churches often have strong opinions and widely divergent expectations for their leaders. Many are tightly tied to certain traditions or ways of doing things.

Church is voluntary. People can vote with their feet or by withholding contributions. This means leaders have to rely on authentic character, which builds trust, which fosters relationships. And relationships are like gardens—they have to be constantly monitored and maintained.

## Relational Mastery Changes Lives

Look at leaders who have a profound impact on people. Better yet, think of the leaders who influenced you early on in your life or ministry. They're likely a big part of the reason you are where you are today.

Though we probably didn't think of it at the time as *emotional intelligence*, there was just something about the way they connected to and inspired us. Perhaps it was the way they understood, challenged, or believed in us. That relational connection ignited something deep within us that we didn't even know was there.

I am convinced that if you had video of some of those interactions, you would see those spiritual leaders and your mentors living out the very skills we've been talking about in these pages. God used his truth and their people skills to attract, influence, mold, and shape you. Don't you want to learn those same skills?

## Relational Mastery Gets Us through Tense or Difficult Situations

Jim could have dug a foxhole and declared war on the board member who was opposing his initiatives. That's what a lot of pastors would do in a similar situation—even though that strategy never turns out well.

Instead, armed with humility and a deeper understanding of his own emotional triggers, Jim decided to be a peacemaker and move toward Greg. He apologized. He tuned in. He listened. His actions were honoring to God. And the men defused a potentially serious conflict.

We have all seen, far too many times, how deep-seated personal or congregational friction can destroy a church. Jim's example shows us that managing conflict wisely can move us past old wounds and stubborn barriers to seasons of unprecedented growth.

## Relational Mastery Matters for Leading Organizational Change and Growth

In any congregation, you'll find a few adventurous souls who love and welcome change. And you'll find a much larger group that resists change and just wants to maintain the status quo. Change makes most people uncomfortable. It is hard. It brings fears, insecurities, and uncertainties to the surface. Leaders who are adept at managing relationships are better aware of these conflicting emotional tensions and are able to navigate them skillfully.

### The Skills of Relational Mastery

Self-aware leaders who enjoy strong relational influence seem to have four skills.

### Skill 1: Building Trust

At the pastors' conference Pastor Susan had an epiphany. She realized that she doesn't really understand her people—and vice versa. They are rural farmers; she's a city girl! Plus, this is her first pastoral assignment.

No wonder people sometimes look at her as if they don't know what she's talking about or where she's coming from!

On her trip home, she remembered two specific invitations to dinner during her first month in town that she had to decline. Reflecting on several other after-church conversations in recent months, she recalled a few comments along the lines of "sure do wish we could get to know you better."

Taking a sip of bottled water, Susan reflected on her decision to spend time getting to know people in light of building trust. She realized that she may have come off as standoffish to this tight knit community. They didn't know that much about her. She decided, *I'm going to ask questions about their lives. Then I'm going to tell them about my life, my childhood, my quirks, my call to ministry.*

Susan not only makes good brownies, she is one smart cookie! Or, she has good instincts. Or, she was paying attention at the conference. Trust is the only sure foundation in leadership. Without trust, nothing you try to build will last. The degree to which people trust you is the degree to which they will be willing to follow you.

Susan's instincts are right. She can build trust only if she will implement five key practices.

### Show Genuine Interest

This means taking time to listen and ask meaningful questions. It means making mental notes (or actual written notes!) of things people say—upcoming events or celebrations, travel plans, birthdays, anniversaries of the deaths of loved ones, prayer concerns, pending medical tests, or whatever.

Then it means checking back at appropriate times to see how those people are doing. These small "check-ins" let people know you were paying attention. It shows them you care.

## Communicate Warmth and Openness

Do you make eye contact? Smile? Turn and face people? Put down your phone? These simple gestures communicate openness and warmth. They send a message: I'm glad to see you. You matter more than the task I'm doing.

## Share Something Personal

People put pastors on pedestals. (Try to say that five times quickly!) Seriously, the crazy misperception of some is that pastors don't struggle with the same problems that "normal people" or "mere mortals" do. Some pastors actually like this lofty status and try to maintain an "above it all" image. But this only breeds distance.

Pedestal pastors might sometimes seem impressive, but they are rarely impactful. Over time they come across as aloof and unapproachable.

Vulnerability is the scarier but better approach. The risk is opening up, being honest, sharing one's struggles. The reward is being known. And the result of being known is trust. Think about it. You only deeply trust people you know well.

This has been one of Susan's big epiphanies—and big challenges. She knows she needs to open up more, be more transparent. And yet she struggles with sharing much about herself. Why? There are several reasons. She's on the introvert end of the personality scale. She also battles perfectionism and fears rejection. Naturally, this combination leaves her reluctant to disclose her own foibles. But post-conference, she's decided to be more open about her struggles.

What she has discovered has amazed her. The more honest she is about her own life—her pain and problems, her flaws and faults—the more comfortable people seem to be around her. Her authenticity hasn't repelled people; it has attracted them! They are starting to feel like they know her and can trust her.

This is what relational mastery involves: sharing windows into your personal and spiritual growth. This sets an example for others. It lets them know that we are all works in progress, all growing together.

## Demonstrate Competence

People trust leaders who know what they are doing and are committed to doing their work with excellence. One way to show this is to engage in leadership development opportunities and talk about what you are learning. This lets people know you take your work seriously, and it breeds trust.

## Communicate Carefully

Dig into most problems and you'll find that much of the trouble can be blamed on noncommunication and/or miscommunication. Good leaders with good relational capital are good communicators. They think of creative ways to talk about vision, plans, finances, and other congregational issues. They make it a priority to be sure people are clear about what's going on. They understand that in a loud, distracting world, people have to hear a message in several different ways and at assorted times for it to stick.

People trust leaders who are transparent, thorough communicators. They feel in the know. Abreast of the what, why, and how of organizational changes, they are more able to participate enthusiastically.

## Reflection Questions

Okay, time to sit back and wrestle with what you have just read.

◉ Whom on your leadership team do you not know or understand as well as you would like? When and how can you engage those individuals to learn more about them and their story?

◉ How susceptible are you to pedestal syndrome? How much pressure do you feel to maintain an image of perfection and aloofness? List three things you could tell about yourself that would help dismantle this image and let others know you better.

◉ Do people tend to open up with you? Do they make themselves vulnerable? Do they show authenticity, airing their own goals, dreams, faults, and failings?

◉ What surprising things are you learning about yourself as you work through the principles of emotional intelligence? What can you share with others about your journey that would be helpful for them to know?

◉ Can you cite any instances recently where feedback suggested people were frustrated by noncommunication or miscommunication with you? What can you do to rectify these situations?

Here is an experiment we mentioned early in the chapter on personal insight, but it bears repeating here because of how effective it can be in building relational trust. Ask three people to give you feedback about your tone of voice, facial expressions, and body language. Ask for suggestions on how you could come across as warmer and more open. Note that it will be easier for others to answer this question than to tell you what you do that *hinders* warmth.

Don't just nod at honest feedback. Implement it!

### Skill 2: Managing Expectations

A second skill of leaders who enjoy productive and fruitful relationships with their teams and congregations is that they have learned to manage expectations. It was researcher T. W. Klink who wrote in 1969 about how vocational ministers function within a network of *unwritten contracts of expectation.*[1]

First, what is an expectation? It's more than a hope or a preference. It's what you anticipate. It's thinking, "This is what will happen or what definitely should happen." Expectations are often reasonable, rooted in unchanging beliefs and values. For example, "Leaders shouldn't lie to their followers!" However, many of our expectations are arbitrary, rooted only in cultural traditions or personal taste, such as, "I think Sunday worship should always include a choir wearing red robes and singing only hymns."

Here is why expectations matter. Whenever a person, event, or thing fails to live up to our expectations, we feel disappointed. And the gap between our expectation and actual experience determines the degree of our disappointment. One of my favorite restaurants used to have stellar food and service. Then suddenly it didn't. I figured they must have a new chef. After several disappointing meals in a row, I decided to forego eating there.

Pastoral leaders who have been around the block a few times understand this expectation-disappointment phenomenon all too well. Everyone has a different idea about how the pastor should go about ministering— how he or she should preach, visit the sick, and on and on. Problem is, most of these expectations are implicit rather than spelled out. The pastor has one set of expectations in his or her head; and the individual members all are working from different sets! What could possibly go wrong?

Everything! Unmet expectations always spark disappointment. Unaddressed, this disappointment can morph into hurt feelings, discontentment, strong feelings of injustice and betrayal, even anger and bitterness. There's no telling how much congregational conflict has its roots right here.

Klink noted that it is only when expectations are stated, understood, and agreed upon, that a minister is in any sort of position to carry out his vocation effectively and with a sense of personal fulfillment.

So how do emotionally intelligent pastors do this? How can you work to spell out expectations proactively and manage them actively? Here are four steps.

## Identify

The obvious first step is to identify expectations, both your own and those of your congregational leaders and members. By the way, the *stated* expectations of a pastoral search committee may not accurately portray the *actual* expectations of the congregation at large. What people say they want and what they really want often do not match. To make matters worse, people oftentimes have no clue what they want. It can sometimes feel like chasing the elusive Bigfoot or shooting at a moving target.

For many, knowing and saying what they *don't* want is easier than spelling out what they do.

## Clarify

Conversations are opportunities to name expectations. By asking good questions, listening carefully, empathizing with concerns, and inviting further dialogue, we can clarify the expectations people hold and be sure we understand. This takes time, but it paves the way for educating others about our leadership and negotiating better agreements.

Pastor Bill is improving at this. Here's one example of how this works on the fly—in the nitty-gritty of everyday ministry.

Mrs. Jones—who has only been at the church a year or so—has just stormed into the church offices and unloaded on Pastor Bill for not caring about her sick husband. Watch how Pastor Bill skillfully applies this second aspect of managing expectations—clarifying—while he assures Mrs. Jones of his genuine care and concern.

........................................................

**Pastor Bill** (taken aback, praying quickly and silently for self-control and a non-defensive spirit, but showing concern): "Oh, Mrs. Jones, come in. Please, sit down and tell me more about how your husband is doing. Also, I want to hear more about why you think I don't care and didn't visit."

[Note: Pastor Bill is *asking*. Moments later in the conversation]:

**Pastor Bill:** "So, it sounds like you were expecting me to visit your husband every day while he was in the hospital."

[Note: Pastor Bill is engaged in *reflective listening*.]

**Mrs. Jones:** "Of course! All my pastors since I was a little girl visited every day. When my momma was ill, Pastor Bob was there every day. I don't know how we would have gotten through it without him. Then when my dear daddy got sick and passed away, Pastor John was our rock. He came every day and prayed with us. And when he couldn't come, he at least called to check on us and to see how I was holding up. As my new pastor, I thought you'd be there every day too. I was really scared that I was going to lose him. And when you weren't there I felt very alone. It just seemed like you didn't care."

**Pastor Bill:** "Oh, Mrs. Jones. I am so sorry to hear that you were feeling all those things. I had no idea. That must have been very scary for you."

[Note: Pastor Bill is *empathizing*.]

**Pastor Bill:** "I want you to know I care very much about your husband and you, and I also believe pastoral visits are very important. I understand this has been a hard and scary time for the both of you. I would never want you to feel abandoned or uncared for by me."

[Note: Pastor Bill is *affirming*.]

**Pastor Bill:** "It sounds like your former pastors visited sick church members daily. That's exemplary, and I'm sure it was very meaningful for you. In my pastorates I have found that two visits a week seems to work well for most members. That allows me to stay in touch without intruding too much. Plus, it allows me to fulfill all my other tasks too. In the future, please know you're *always* welcome to call me and ask for extra visits. I'm glad to come whenever I can."

**Mrs. Jones:** "So, not all pastors make daily visits?"

**Pastor Bill:** "Actually, from my interactions with colleagues in ministry, I've found my visitation schedule to be about the norm. There are some pastors in smaller churches who can still visit daily. There are others, in larger churches with a lot of older members, who are only able to visit once a week. It varies from church to church, and pastor to pastor.

[Note: Pastor Bill is *educating*.]

**Mrs. Jones:** "Oh, I guess I hadn't thought about all that."

**Pastor Bill:** "Mrs. Jones, I want to thank you for bringing this to my attention. It makes me wonder if maybe other folks in our body have similar concerns. Anyway, I'm glad we were able to talk. I do care. And I'm here for you. Anytime you have a concern, I want you to feel free to contact me. Can I pray for you and your husband right now?"

[Note: Pastor Bill *thanks* Mrs. Jones for her feedback and *invites* future feedback.]

Do you see all the wise things Pastor Bill did? He . . .

◉ Asked open-ended questions
◉ Listened carefully to identify expectations
◉ Affirmed underlying concerns
◉ Educated his new parishioner regarding his own rationale and expectations
◉ Thanked Mrs. Jones for bringing this matter to his attention
◉ Invited further conversation.
◉ Brilliant!

Emotionally intelligent pastors enjoy healthy relationships, in part because they manage expectations.

If we don't let people know what they can realistically expect from our leadership, they will create their own set of expectations—ill-informed, unrealistic ones. These expectations will come from their prior experiences, their own values and desires, things they have read or heard about, or ideas they just concocted out of thin air.

## Educate

By sharing what people can expect from you early on in your pastorate, you spare yourself and your people unpleasant surprises and heartache later down the road.

Here are just a few topics you will need to discuss with your board and congregation:

- Your personal philosophy of ministry
- Your vision (in other words, your holy hopes and dreams for your people)
- Your focus and priorities
- Your values
- Your strengths and weaknesses
- What you do differently than others

Imagine, for example, you are a gifted teacher. Your passion is to go verse-by-verse through books of the Bible, helping people understand essential Christian doctrine and disciplines. The dynamic, topical preaching style of your predecessor just isn't your strength.

Making sure the congregation knows this up front is crucial. Helping them see the need for your style can help reduce future complaints, criticisms, and conflict. Some members may even come to see your approach as a real asset and learn to value its importance.

If you're not proactive in this way, if you just let folks "figure it out themselves" over time without the benefit of your rationale and perspective, disappointment and dissatisfaction are sure to follow. Eventually you will hear whispers: "Why doesn't the new pastor preach the same kind of exciting messages that Pastor So-and-So did?"

## Negotiate

Talk about *everything*. Start conversations about frequency of hospital visitation, office hours, availability during evening hours, church vision (what we're about and why) and ministry strategies (how we will carry out our mission), time off, continuing education, and congregational expectations of spouses and children. These are but a few issues that should be brought out into the open and negotiated. Even if resolution isn't immediate, broaching these subjects and actively discussing them is healthy. You, your board, and your congregants will all benefit.

## Reflection Questions

Here are some questions to help you think about how you are currently doing with managing expectations and areas in which you might improve.

- To what degree do you sense the members of your church have unrealistic expectations of your pastoral ministry?
- What do you think these wrong expectations are?
- What do you see as your unique strengths, your weaknesses, and special areas of focus in your ministry? Have you educated people about these? When and how will you do so?
- What expectations do you have for your leadership and congregants? What disappointments have you had in regard to these expectations? How has this affected you emotionally?
- What are some specific ways you could strategically and positively have conversations about these expectations?

## Skill 3: Empowering Others

A third practice of pastoral leaders who enjoy energizing ministry relationships rather than de-energizing ones is making a mental shift to empowering others. This is another way of saying that they embrace the teaching of Ephesians 4:12—that pastors are called "to equip [God's] people for works of service, so that the body of Christ may be built up."

## Developing an Empowering Mind-Set

Do you have any idea what might happen if you developed a ministry mind-set among your staff and leadership team that said, "We're not going to have a church where only the 'pros' (ordained clergy) are expected and allowed to serve. We're going to decentralize the ministry and 'give it away.' We're going to help every believer figure out how he or she is gifted. Then we're going to equip and prepare folks—and encourage them—to use their gifts to bless others."

I can tell you what would happen. You'd have the beginnings of a ministry revolution! Spectators tend towards criticism, while participants tend towards promotion! I have heard it said that "spectators become critics, but participants become boosters!"[2]

The old hierarchal system, where leadership flows from the top downward, is dead. It only breeds disinterest among the body and burnout among the staff. What if you turned this unworkable model upside down? What if you focused more on growing and unleashing your lay leaders and regular members?

It's a huge mind-set shift, that's for sure. Your leadership would have to take on more of an empowering, facilitating, equipping role. Instead of "hoarding the ministry," you would be sharing. But the benefits are incalculable. People who are involved feel invested. They take ownership. Everyone—not just a select few—works together for a common goal. You would unleash a small army of gifted people! Leaders who do this invariably have healthier churches than leaders who muzzle their members and restrict involvement.

What would it look like to empower your leadership team? Your church members?

*You would be discipling people like Jesus did.* He trained the ordinary men and women who followed him—then unleashed them to change the world.

*You would encourage awareness and use of spiritual gifts.* Through experimentation and observation, believers would begin to see the unique ways God has wired them to make an eternal difference in the church and the world.

*You would find yourself open to new ideas.* Perhaps a member shares that he or she is concerned about helping the homeless in your city. Maybe this is God's way of leading your church into a vibrant ministry with "the least of these" (see Matt. 25:40). Savvy leaders encourage this kind of dialogue and help members figure out constructive ways to explore possible callings.

*You would be sharing power.* It can feel risky and be scary to allow people to try new things. However, good leaders fight the temptation to micromanage. Instead, they offer support, as needed.

*You would affirm and encourage.* The most beloved and most effective leaders constantly encourage others to try new things. Maybe you sense that a timid, spiritually sensitive young person could do a great job with Scripture reading before the Sunday message. Who knows? Something as small as providing a simple opportunity and giving lots of encouragement just might spark a lifetime of faithful service!

*You would discover budding teachers, pastors, and evangelists.* Good leaders are observant and they are always looking for and recruiting the next wave—or generation—of leaders. They work to replace themselves. Whom do you see with gifts that just need development?

*You would challenge people to take the next step.* Consider how Pastor Joe simultaneously affirmed and challenged his young youth pastor.

........................................................

**Pastor Joe:** Bucky *(Why is it that youth pastors always have cool names like Bucky or Rocky or Clint or Rip?)*, I want you to know that I've noticed how hard you've been working to engage our youth. You've handled several situations really well. When those parents challenged you the other day in your youth parents' meeting, you didn't react defensively.

In fact, it was amazing how you turned that situation around. I am so impressed!

[Note: Pastor Joe is using *affirmation*.]

**Pastor Joe:** I also notice, though, that you have been working long hours—almost killing yourself—to pull off all these youth events. Meanwhile, I'm pretty sure we have some young adults who would be willing to help you. That could be a win-win. Getting them involved would lighten your load and help them grow as well. I wonder, what are some ways you could fold those adults into the youth ministry?

[Note: Pastor Joe is issuing a *challenge*.]

I know this kind of thing is risky and messy. When we entertain the bold idea of equipping others for ministry, we immediately encounter obstacles, don't we? Some of these obstacles are internal and some are external. Do any of these look familiar?

- Fear of or resistance to change
- Fear of losing control
- Concern that others won't do things exactly the way you would do them (News flash: They won't. Their efforts may not be as good; or they might be better!)
- It takes time and effort to train others. (Once people are trained, however, it's like you've multiplied yourself. The time saving on the back end is enormous!)
- There aren't a lot of ministry models of equipping churches to emulate.

If you sense some of these obstacles in yourself, it will help to go back and reread the chapters on personal insight and personal mastery. These chapters will help you learn the internal skills needed to unleash the power of the people around you.

## Reflection Questions

Now let's look at some personal reflection questions about empowering others.

- Where do you see your congregation and especially your leaders in terms of discipleship? Are they maturing followers of Jesus? In what specific ways can you foster spiritual growth and passion in your congregation? Among your leaders?
- Think about the individuals who helped you identify your call to ministry and development as a leader. What things did they do that really helped? In what ways can you duplicate what they did as you seek to develop others in your ministry?
- What internal obstacles (such as fear of losing control, busyness) could get in the way of your empowering those in your ministry? How can you address these obstacles?
- Whom in your ministry could use some loving feedback to spur their growth? What specifically can you say to affirm them? What challenge could you give them?

## Skill 4: Managing Conflict

A fourth practice of leaders who enjoy healthy ministry relationships is the ability to navigate conflict successfully.

If you've ever been involved in any kind of serious church conflict, well, God bless you! Few things are uglier. You know all too well how emotions—others' as well as your own—can get out of control. Obstinate board members, threatening donors, jealous staffers, wounded parishioners, angry factions—these kinds of tense relationships are common, even among the people of God, and addressing them is not for the squeamish.

Denied or ignored, however, resentments can morph into rage, and slights, whether real or imagined, can lead to splits. Think of how many church members you know who still carry wounds from previous church conflicts. Think of those surveys of pastors who have left vocational ministry, and the fact that unresolved or unrelenting conflict is often listed as a primary reason for the decision to transition to another career.

What does the Bible say?

Jesus said, "Blessed are the peacemakers, for they will be called children of God" (Matt. 5:9). The apostle Paul told the Roman believers, "If it is possible, as far as it depends on you, live at peace with everyone" (Rom. 12:18). Later, he told his protégé Timothy, "And the Lord's servant must not be quarrelsome but must be kind to everyone, able to teach, not resentful" (2 Tim. 2:24). Elsewhere, the New Testament warns, "Watch out that no poisonous root of bitterness grows up to trouble you, corrupting many" (Heb. 12:15 NLT).

Scripture is clear: Christlike leaders make it a top priority to address conflict with humility, grace, and truth. Since the gospel is fundamentally about reconciliation, gospel-centered ministry will always seek to avoid unnecessary conflict and resolve existing tensions.

Still, it's hard. Who relishes conflict, other than a few odd souls who seem to thrive on drama? Truth be told, most pastors—most people— dread conflict like the plague. We go into ministry in order to "help and serve," not spend our days dodging bullets!

We are left with these truths: conflict is inevitable. It's a fact of life in a fallen world. But learning to manage it healthily is not only possible, it can make a huge difference in ministry. Our goal isn't the absence of conflict. That would be the height of unrealistic expectations. Our goal should be learning how to engage in healthy, nondestructive conflict.

## Understanding Conflict

One simple definition of conflict is "opposing or incompatible actions, objectives or ideas."[3]

This is an unavoidable reality—even among Christians. How could it be otherwise? We are all unique. We all have our own thoughts and perspectives, likes and dislikes, preferences and plans. None of us are fully sanctified yet (see Phil. 1:6). Our minds aren't yet fully renewed (see Rom. 12:2). Therefore, conflict occurs, in some form or another, in all close relationships. A marriage, family, or friendship without some sort of conflict is either in a state of estrangement or disengagement.

There are different kinds of conflict. *Overt* conflict[4] is expressed. It is outward, obvious to all. It may arise in the form of polite verbal criticism; an off-handed, loaded comment; an opposing opinion, or a hostile argument.

*Latent* conflict[5] is conflict that lurks below the surface. It is not expressed outwardly—or at least not in a clear and direct manner. Friendly resistance to a plan, an irritated tone, a terse response, a passive-aggressive refusal to return calls, texts, or emails—all of these may be indicative of latent tensions. Even unnamed and unacknowledged, the influence of such hidden conflict can be felt. Festering beneath the surface like a quiet-but-active volcano, it may gain strength and explode violently without notice. Occasionally latent conflict simply evaporates—as misconceptions are shown to be false or as individuals grow in the faith.

## Roots of Conflict

When people are driven by pride or selfishness, they tend to ride roughshod over others to get whatever they want. When others become afraid of losing face, control, or position, or when they fear being taken advantage of, they become defensive and belligerent. Thus, most conflict, and surely all destructive conflict, involves some level of mistrust and misunderstanding. The parties dig in their heels and engage in a fierce power struggle. Who will give in first? Which side will get its way?

Then, if there's a history between the parties, some conflicts are exacerbated by a sinful desire to pay back the other for past hurts or slights.

### "BUT I HATE CONFLICT!"

I hear you! But ignoring it, denying it, or running from it doesn't make it go away.

If you hate conflict as much as I do, you might be interested in knowing how I acquired more emotional intelligence in this area. I will tell you upfront that it was not easy!

In short, I did two things: I learned, and I practiced.

I learned every communication and conflict negotiation skill I could. I read books and articles. I attended seminars. I wrestled with the principles in this book. I talked to skilled practitioners in the delicate, rare art of conflict resolution. Then . . .

I practiced those skills every time conflict reared its nerve-wracking head. I took the time to write out what happened. I analyzed each situation. Then I spent time forming better, more appropriate responses. I did much of this after the initial conflict. By doing so, I was at least more prepared the next time a similar tension arose.

Practice is the key. Learning about managing conflict is good, but it isn't enough. In the same way that you can't learn to ride a bike simply by reading a book or watching a video, you can't learn to manage conflict that way either. I had to lean into conflict, wade into actual, real-life tension, not run from it. I had to practice healthy communication and conflict management skills. Only then did I begin to achieve proficiency. Only then did I begin to feel more in control of myself in tense situations. I often found sweet peace on the other side of tough conversations. Another benefit was that I became more objective and able to take criticism less personally.

If I can learn such a skill, anyone can. And if such a skill could lead to better relational interactions for me, it can do the same for you.

The point here isn't to psychoanalyze those embroiled in feuds. It is simply to say that misunderstandings, when discussed, can result in deeper understanding. When there is no attempt to understand and defuse tension, look out!

So what can we do about conflict? Plenty!

Some conflicts can be prevented altogether. They are avoidable. How? You head them off at the pass by taking proactive measures. You work to establish trust, create realistic expectations, and communicate carefully.

Most conflicts have to be managed. By listening, taking pains to clarify different points of view, understanding and analyzing tensions so as to determine a productive and healthy way forward, you can avoid unnecessary grief.

The good news and great power of the gospel is that all conflicts can be leveraged for growth! Our God is redemptive. He specializes in bringing good out of bad. He doesn't waste *anything*, ever.

A church in Louisiana had an ugly split in 1995, leaving two deeply wounded, disillusioned congregations. Fifteen years later, the Lord humbled the leaders of these two factions, and convicted them of their need to go back and confess their pride to one another and seek forgiveness. They returned to the very building in which they'd had some of their most heated and angry arguments, sat in a circle, and took turns confessing their wrong words and actions. The result? Much-needed healing, and the merging of the two congregations back into one church! There's no conflict that the gospel of Jesus can't heal!

## Six Ways to Manage Conflict

Let's wrap up this discussion with six powerful leadership reminders for managing conflict in a God-honoring, people-blessing way:

*Manage your mind-set.* Instead of seeing conflict as a battle to be won, a threat, or a potential disaster, see it as a problem to be solved, a challenge, a potential blessing. Take captive any negative thoughts (see

2 Cor. 10:5) that characterize the "others" as "enemies." These perspectives will only promote defensiveness and anger within you. Instead, try to envision others as concerned, threatened, or hurt. Seek to win *them*, not some silly argument!

*Master your emotions.* "The fruit of the Spirit is . . . self-control" (Gal. 5:22–23). Ask for divine power to avoid knee-jerk reactions and harsh words you will regret later. Better to say nothing or "I need to think about all that and get back to you later." Call time-out when you find your emotions strong.

*Listen, more than anything.* Get your "yeses." Use reflective listening to let the other party know that you are hearing them. Give them ample opportunities to clarify their message. Paraphrase or restate to others what you hear them saying. Don't give up until they can say, "Yes. *That* is what I mean."

*Analyze the conflict.* Reflect before responding. Ask lots of questions. Ask God for insight. Keep in mind the two watchwords—prayerful and careful. Remember that overt or expressed conflict is like an iceberg; you are only seeing what's above the waterline. The biggest part of the conflict likely lies under the surface. Go deep!

*Determine your response.* Strategize on the best option for responding. Forecast possible outcomes for each strategy or communication you think of. Again, ask God for wisdom and help. Then determine what you will say or do.

*Obtain outside help when needed.* Proverbs 15:22 says, "Plans fail for lack of counsel, but with many advisers they succeed." Don't be too proud to ask for help, to solicit wisdom from older mentors or more seasoned leaders. If the stakes are high and you cannot get past an impasse, seek mediation.

## Managing Conflict Activity

Here's an activity you can do to bring clarity to a conflict you are seeking to manage.

- Describe a current or past conflict situation.
- Describe the tip of the iceberg (surface issue).
- Write out the exact words that were said by all parties as best as you can recall.
- Describe any relevant historical context.
- Discuss underlying issues, what's going on under the surface with key parties, as best you can determine.
- Discuss your thoughts, feelings, reactions, or what goes on inside you when you think about this situation.
- Discuss possible communications, strategies, or interventions you could use in this situation and seek the best ways to respond.
- Name a leader you could discuss this situation with and from whom you could solicit feedback.

### *Toward Greater Relational Mastery*

Remember the guy I mentioned who quipped that *people* were his biggest problem? The ministry doesn't have to be that way. People can actually be a source of great joy. Relationships in the church can be immensely gratifying.

Relational mastery is what sets apart the average leader from true, transformational leaders. They have greater impact because they have greater emotional intelligence. If you work to develop the skills we have talked about here—and practice them until they become habits—you can be a transformational leader too. People will be drawn to you because you are more authentic, engaging, and healthy.

As a bonus, you will be less frustrated and more energized. Trust me, nothing is more de-energizing than trying to pull off a one-man or one-woman ministry show in a church culture filled with mistrust, unrealistic expectations, and constant conflict.

The fact that you have read this far likely shows a hunger to learn and a humble heart. Whatever your calling, gifts, training, or experience, I know this: If you'll devote yourself to developing the habits we've discussed in these pages, you'll have the people skills needed to lead others to new levels of growth and joy.

These aren't just words—you have what it takes. You *can* do this. Why not now?

I believe in you—and more importantly, God does. Will you let him use you in big, new ways?

## PART 4

# *Further Application*

# Where Are They Now?
# (Susan, Bill, and Jim Revisited)

Six months after their big pastors' conference on emotional intelligence, Susan, Jim, and Bill are participating in another conference: an hour-long conference *call*. They have done this at two-month intervals to compare notes, commiserate over struggles, celebrate successes, and basically just encourage one another in the ongoing quest to become EI-savvy leaders.

In their first call, the trio discussed Travis Bradberry and Jean Greaves' popular book *Emotional Intelligence 2.0* (which they had all agreed to read following the conference). Also in that call, Jim shared about his efforts to repair and reset his relationship with Greg and the board. He talked about how tense and awkward their first couple of meetings were, but then how—through lots of intentionality—the two leaders had actually been able to forge the beginnings of a real friendship! Ironically, when Jim had humbly shared some of the insights he'd discovered at the conference, Greg had expressed a need for some of those same EI leadership skills in his own life! The men started meeting weekly to discuss another emotional intelligence book—and how those ideas could be put to use in the marketplace and the church.

In Jim's words, "The board got so encouraged by the radical change in my relationship with Greg that a new spirit of trust began to permeate the entire leadership team. Vision and passion started growing. The staff got engaged. I really feel hopeful. It's funny, as I've worked to listen more and 'power up' less, I feel like my influence has grown exponentially. Even my wife told me the other day, 'I think you listen better since that conference.' Of course, I couldn't resist saying, 'What, dear? Did you just say something?'"

Jim told Bill in an email a few weeks later, "I think I'm finally realizing the difference between driving the flock and leading the sheep."

In their four-month conference call, Susan and Jim focused mostly on Bill, who had been fairly quiet in the first call. They wanted to know how he was doing in his battle against burnout.

Bill shared that in the four months since the conference, he'd been seeing a counselor weekly—three sessions a month by himself and one meeting a month with his wife. "That's been really helpful in unearthing some of the core issues behind all my people-pleasing." Bill reported that he and Celeste had also taken a week-long vacation in which he didn't check email even one time and answered only one church-related phone call. "And you know what? The world kept spinning, and I slept about ten hours a day, and it was wonderful."

Bill added that he'd been taking a strict day off each Monday. "I told my secretary, board, and staff that unless it's a serious emergency, I am *unreachable*. Do not call! On that day, I have no agenda. I might get up and go fishing—I've done that three or four times. Haven't caught much, but it's been fun. Some days I read, but only fun stuff, like fiction or history—no ministry books. I've taken naps and I've sat in our back-porch swing and watched the birds and squirrels. Then—and this is big—every Monday night Celeste and I have started going on a *real live actual date*! We have two rules on date night: phones off and no shoptalk. That's been *so* good."

Susan and Jim were amazed, but Bill wasn't done. "I've also started walking and journaling, not every day, but most mornings. At work, I still often feel a twinge of guilt when I say no to a request, but I'm realizing that I can only do what I can do. And it seems like when I start to go into a funk over some criticism, I catch myself quicker—and turn off all the negative chatter in my head. I don't ever want to go back to the way I used to live!" ·

Now, in their six-month post-conference catch-up, Susan was the one asking for counsel. She'd seen enormous changes in her attitude toward the church and the congregation's attitude toward her. Despite the fact that a couple of older families did leave the church, multiple younger families had started coming. As Susan consistently put herself out there, people had responded in good ways. The rural farming community of Claymore felt very much like home to the "girl from the city."

"So here's my dilemma," Susan said. "I just got an email from my district office that there's an opening at a church up the street from one of the larger college campuses in Illinois. And there's a kind of renaissance taking place in the college ministry at that church.

"I've always had a heart for college students. I just feel like those years are such a critical time in a kid's life—they were for me. Young adults are wrestling with all of life's big questions: What do I believe? What am I going to do with my life? Who am I going to spend my life with? Plus, you've got international students right there, from all over the world. I mean, you can have a global impact and never leave your zip code!

"So, I don't know. I love my congregation and Claymore *so* much. The thought of packing up and leaving makes me sad, but this would be my dream situation: ministering to university students. And, we found out there's a high school there looking for a men's basketball coach. Plus, it would put us close to family."

Jim and Bill listened and asked questions. Susan was clearly torn.

Susan continued. "I know this: my time in Kansas has helped me learn how to connect with people who are really different from me. I'd like to think my emotional intelligence is greater now than it was a year ago."

Bill piped up, "Susan, I don't interact with you every day, but just in the six months I've known you, I've seen you grow so much. You are brave and humble and smart as a whip. Heck, I wish I could hire you to come work with college students here in Nashville! Look, I know this: If you stay where you are, you'll just keep improving as a leader and keep blessing the socks off those folks in Claymore. And if you leave, you can do so with your head held high. You've been a good and faithful servant to that flock."

Jim had strong thoughts about what Susan should do, but as he considered what to say, he got the sense he was not supposed to say anything. And so, he didn't—a sign of his own growth. He and Bill agreed to pray for Susan until the following Tuesday afternoon—that was her deadline.

"Can we do a quick conference call at the end of the day on Tuesday?" Bill asked. "Just so we can celebrate with you—whatever your decision?"

"Perfect!" Susan replied. "I'd love that."

# The Long-Term Implications of Emotional Intelligence: A Manifesto

Manifesto is a strong word. Maybe when you hear it you think of an intense speaker in a sweltering auditorium screaming into a microphone and working up a boisterous crowd. Or you envision some kind of activist fanatic nailing a list of demands to the front door of City Hall. In truth, a manifesto is just a declaration of aims and principles. It's a statement that answers the all-important question, "So what?" or maybe, "Now what?" That's the gist of this final chapter. I present a manifesto I hope you will embrace.

What are the logical implications of emotional intelligence for Christian leaders? What should we do with this much-needed knowledge that has a proven power to transform both leaders and churches?

With all my heart, I believe the following principles and practices of emotional intelligence should mark the church. We owe it to God to do everything with excellence! We owe it to those we serve to serve them well. We owe it to ourselves to become all that God wants us to be. Will you join me in the following commitments?

## *Implications for Pastors*

◉ As a pastor, I will make it a priority to grow in emotional and relational skills. With God's help, I will study EI concepts and incorporate into my life the EI skills and habits discussed in this book.

◉ As a pastor, I will model emotionally intelligent leadership.

## Implications for Denominational Leaders

◉ As a denominational leader, I will seek out ways to help educate lay leaders and congregations regarding the nature of modern pastoral ministry. I will foster and referee, if necessary, needed conversations about ministerial stress and burnout.

◉ As a denominational leader, I will work to help lay leaders negotiate and honor reasonable expectations between their congregation and their pastor.

◉ As a denominational leader, I will work to better equip pastors and congregations at resolving interpersonal conflicts and navigating seasons of change.

◉ As a denominational leader, I will demonstrate emotional intelligence in my own leadership and encourage pastors under my care to develop their emotional intelligence skills.

## Implications for Seminaries and Bible Schools

◉ As a seminary administrator or department head, I will seek to make the study and discussion of emotional intelligence part of our regular ministry training curriculum. I will redouble my efforts to make sure that our graduates are "people smart" and not just "Bible smart."

◉ As a professor, I will use my platform, influence, and class time to help students grasp the important truths and skills of emotional intelligence.

## *Implications for All Christians in All Walks of Life*

⦿ As a follower of Jesus Christ, I will pursue—and strive to model—emotionally intelligent leadership in all my interactions and relationships. As a parent, student, sibling, employee, boss, neighbor, colleague, or team member, I will make it my aim to follow the beautiful example of Christ described in Philippians—living humbly and with an others-centered, servant mind-set.

**Signed** _____

**Dated** _____

# *Notes*

## Chapter 2

1. Jeannie Clarkson, "Pastoral Burnout: The Results of a Study Examining the Relationships of Emotional Intelligence and Performance Based Self-Esteem with Burnout among Pastors" (PhD diss., Walden University, 2013), 158–76.

2. Dean R. Hoge and Jacqueline E. Wenger, *Pastors in Transition: Why Clergy Leave Local Church Ministry* (Grand Rapids, MI: Eerdmans, 2005), 76.

3. Thom S. Rainer, "How Many Hours Must a Pastor Work," Thom S. Rainer: Growing Healthy Churches Together, July 24, 2013, https://thom-rainer.com/2013/07/how-many-hours-must-a-pastor-work-to-satisfy-the-congregation/, accessed May 24, 2019.

4. Rae Jean Proeschold-Bell and Sara LeGrand, "High Rates of Obesity and Chronic Disease among United Methodist Clergy," in *Obesity* 18, no. 9 (2010), 1867–70.

5. Jeannie Clarkson, "Pastoral Burnout," Executive Summary, www.jeannie-millerclarkson.com/research, accessed May 24, 2019.

## Chapter 3

1. Robert J. Sternberg, *Cognitive Psychology 4th ed.* (Belmont, CA: Wadsworth, 2006), 488, 490.

2. Edward L. Thorndike, "Intelligence and its uses" in *Harper's Magazine* (January 1920), 140, 227–235.

3. Howard Gardner, *Frames of Mind: The Theory of Multiple Intelligences* (New York, NY: Basic Books, Inc., 1983), 73–276.

4. *Educational Leadership,* vol 43, no. 2 (October 1985): 50.

5. Peter Salovey and John D. Mayer, "Emotional Intelligence," *Imagination, Cognition and Personality* 9, no. 3 (March 1990), 185–211.

6. Dana L. Joseph and Daniel A. Newman. "Emotional Intelligence: An Integrative Meta-Analysis and Cascading Model." The Journal of Applied Psychology, 2010, 95 (1), 54–78, https://doi.org/10.1037/a0017286.

7. Cary Cherniss and Daniel Goleman, ed. "An EI-based theory of performance" in *The Emotionally Intelligent Workplace: How to Select for, Measure, and Improve Emotional Intelligence in Individuals, Groups, and Organizations* (San Francisco, CA: Jossey-Bass, 2001), 27–44.

8. Geoff Ryan, Lyle M. Spencer, Urs Bernhard, (2012) "Development and validation of a customized competency-based questionnaire: Linking social, emotional, and cognitive competencies to business unit profitability," *Cross Cultural Management: An International Journal*, Journal 19, no. 1 (2012), 90–103, https://doi.org/10.1108/13527601211195646.

9. Troy Heffernan, Grant O'Neill, Tony Travaglione, Marcelle Droulers, (2008) "Relationship marketing: The impact of emotional intelligence and trust on bank performance," *International Journal of Bank Marketing*, Journal 26, no. 3, 183–199, https://doi.org/10.1108/02652320810864652.

10. Marie J. Hayes and Michio Fukumizu, s.v. "Neonate, " in *Encyclopedia of Human Development*, edited by Neil J. Salkind (Thousand Oaks, CA: SAGE Publications, 2005), 904, https://doi.org/10.4135/9781412952484.n439, accessed June 2019.

11. Paul Dumouchel, "Biological Modules and Emotions," *Canadian Journal of Philosophy* 36, sup1(2006), 115–34, doi.org/10.1353/cjp.2007.0036, accessed June 2019.

12. Bogdan Draganski et al., "Neuroplasticity: Changes in Gray Matter Induced by Training," *Nature* 427, no. 6972 (2004), 311–12.

13. Thomas F. Münte et al, "The Musician's Brain as a Model of Neuroplasticity," *Nature Reviews Neuroscience* 3, (2002), 473.

## Chapter 4

1. "Reading Habits of Today's Pastors," June 3, 2013, *Barna Group*, www.barna.com/research/reading-habits-of-todays-pastors, accessed May 17, 2019.

2. "Charles Spurgeon Quotes," BrainyQuote.com, www.brainyquote.com/quotes/charles_spurgeon_181475, accessed May 17, 2019.

3. James E. White, "The Four Steps for Leading Change," February 11, 2016, Church and Culture, www.churchandculture.org/blog/2016/2/11/

the-four-steps-for-leading-change?rq=people%20will%20not%20even%20consider%20change, accessed May 15, 2019.

4. Jared Roth, "The Relationship between Emotional Intelligence and Pastor Leadership in Turnaround Churches" (EdD diss., Pepperdine University, 2011), http://search.proquest.com/openview/95763cb757dac341f5f4646fbdc2544f/1?pq-origsite=gscholar&cbl=18750&diss=y, accessed May 24, 2019.

5. Charles Crismier, "The Significance of Serving," *Charisma Leader*, January 2001, http://ministrytodaymag.com/outreach/service/830-the-significance-of-serving, accessed May 3, 2019.

6. Stephanie Pappas, "Loneliness Is Bad for Your Health, Study Suggests," *Live Science*, January 20, 2013, www.livescience.com/26431-loneliness-harms-health-immune-system.html, accessed May 3, 2019.

## Chapter 5

1. "New Study Shows Nice Guys Finish First," *American Management Association*, January 24, 2019, www.amanet.org/training/articles/new-study-shows-nice-guys-finish-first.aspx?pcode=XCRP, accessed June 2019.

2. "Benjamin Franklin Quotes," BrainyQuote.com, www.brainyquote.com/quotes/benjamin_franklin_151641, accessed May 17, 2019.

3. Carl Jung quoted in Seth M. "20 Carl Jung Quotes That Will Make You Think," *Intellectual Takeout: A Refuge for Rational Discourse*, May 11, 2016, www.intellectualtakeout.org/blog/20-carl-jung-quotes-will-make-you-think, accessed May 24, 2019.

4. Sun Tzu, *The Art of War: The Oldest Military Treatise in the World*, translated from Chinese by Lionel Giles (1910), (e-book, NuVision, 2004), 14.

5. Abraham H. Maslow, *Motivation and Personality*, (Abraham Maslow Publisher, 1970), 158–59, walker.org.uk/pubsebooks/pdfs/Motivation_and_Personality-Maslow.pdf, accessed May 24, 2019.

6. Howard G. Hendricks, *As Iron Sharpens Iron: Building Character in a Mentoring Relationship* (Chicago: Moody Press, 1995), 61.

## Chapter 6

1. Harry S. Truman, Harry S. Truman Presidential Library and Museum, retrieved from www.trumanlibrary.org/whistlestop/study_collections/trumanpapers/psf/longhand/index.php?documentVersion=both&documentid=hst-psf_naid735210-01&pagenumber=3, accessed June 2019.

2. Stephen Covey, *The 7 Habits of Highly Effective People: Powerful Lessons in Personal Change* (New York, NY: Free Press, 2004), 72.

3. Albert Ellis, *Reason and Emotion in Psychotherapy* (New York: Birch Lane Press, 1994), 20–21.

4. Robert McGee, *The Search for Significance* (Nashville: Thomas Nelson, 2003), 18.

### Chapter 7

1. Ed Stetzer, "Engaging an Ever-Changing Culture with a Never-Changing Gospel," August 1, 2014, *The Exchange with Ed Stetzer, Christianity Today*, www.christianitytoday.com/edstetzer/2014/june/avoiding-church-culture-pendulum-swings-engaging-ever-chang.html, accessed May 22, 2019.

2. Stephen R. Covey, "Habit 5: Seek First to Understand, Then to Be Understood," *Franklin Covey*, www.franklincovey.com/the-7-habits/habit-5. html, accessed May 18, 2019.

### Chapter 8

1. T. W. Klink, "The Ministry as Career and Crisis," *Pastoral Psychology* 20, no. 6 (1969): 13–19, https://doi.org/10.1007/BF01785142.

2. James N. Britton, "Viewpoints: The Distinction between Participant and Spectator Role Language in Research and Practice," *Research in the Teaching of English* 18, no. 3 (1984), 320–31, http://www.jstor.org/stable/40171022.3.

3. Conflict. (n.d.). In Alleydog.com's online glossary, www.alleydog.com/glossary/definition.php?term=Conflict, accessed June 23, 2019.

4. Louis R. Pondy, "Organizational Conflict: Concepts and Models," *Administrative Science Quarterly* 12, no. 2 (September 1967), 296, doi. org/10.2307/2391553, accessed June 2019.

5. Pondy, "Organizational Conflict."

# Additional Resources

Get additional free information to assist in your
personal development!

www.JeannieMillerClarkson.com/news

**Thriving Clergy**
sponsored by
Education and Clergy Development, The Wesleyan Church
and Thrive Financial Initiative

*At Full Strength: Navigating the Risks All Pastors Face* by Denny Howard with Hugh White (Indianapolis, IN: Wesleyan Publishing House, 2019).

*Hope for Pastors: A Collaborative Approach to Clergy Financial Health* by Mark A. Rennaker, PhD (Indianapolis, IN: Wesleyan Publishing House, 2016).

**For more information**
www.wesleyan.org/thrivingclergy
www.wphstore.com

# About the Author

**Dr. Jeannie Clarkson** is the researcher behind a study linking emotional intelligence and performance-based self-esteem with burnout among Christian pastors. She is the founder of Christian Care Connection, a multi-staff professional counseling center in the greater Toledo, Ohio, area.

Jeannie is known as a counselor, entrepreneur, and leader in the local Christian community. Christian Care Connection, launched in 2000, provides distinctively professional Christian counseling. Jeannie's heart for pastors led her to join the South Monroe County Ministerial Association where she was elected president three years consecutively, 2005–2008.

Jeannie is a licensed psychologist and licensed professional counselor.

Her academic credentials include a bachelor of biblical studies from East Coast Bible College (now Lee University), a master of arts in counseling from the University of North Carolina at Charlotte, and a doctorate in psychology counseling from Walden University.